COLLINS GEM

HOLIDAY

Group

HarperCollins*Publishers*

HarperCollins Publishers
P. O. Box, Glasgow G4 0NB

A Diagram Book first created by Diagram Visual Information
Limited of 195 Kentish Town Road, London NW5 8SY

First published 1993

Reprint 10 9 8 7 6 5 4 3 2 1 0

© Diagram Visual Information Limited 1993

ISBN 0 00 470280 8
Printed in Great Britain by
HarperCollins Manufacturing, Glasgow

Introduction

Most of us soon tire of doing nothing while on holiday, especially once sightseeing and sunbathing pall. To help you to keep boredom at bay, a collection of enjoyable activities to play on the beach, in parks or accessible fields and woods has been included in one handy volume: *Collins Gem Holiday Games*.

Most of the games can be played by children over the age of five and by adults of any age. Some of them have been used by the Scout and Guide movements. The few pieces of equipment that a selection of the activities require can be taken on holiday or easily obtained; many require no equipment at all.

Many of the outdoor games can be adapted for indoor spaces, such as church halls, schools or club rooms. Wherever played, the area should be clear of obstacles which could be a danger to players involved in running, jumping and making body contact.

Care must be taken not to allow the more spirited players to dominate a group, and sometimes disputes or cheating may arise. A person who is respected, therefore, should be selected as an adjudicator.

Created by the Diagram Group, *Collins Gem Holiday Games* is an attractive companion volume to the same team's *Gem Travel Games*, *Card Games*, *Games For One* and *Card Games 2*.

4

Contents

1. CHASING AND HUNTING GAMES

2. THROWING AND AIMING GAMES

3. RACING GAMES

4. COLLECTING GAMES

5. GUESSING AND REMEMBERING GAMES

6. PRETENDING GAMES

1. Chasing and hunting games

SINGLE FOOTBALL

Number This game is for four or more of any age.

Place and time You can play this outdoors where there is a lengthy play area of at least 30 metres. It is best played in dry weather.

Equipment One large, soft ball and a post are needed. The post could be a stick set in the ground or an existing post, pole, tree, rock or bollard.

Preparation A starting line is marked with chalk on the ground at the opposite end of the play area from the post.

How to play ▶ One player is chosen to be the runner. The rest are fielders. ▶ The runner stands behind the starting line with the ball. The fielders may

stand anywhere (**A**). ▶ When she is ready, the runner throws the ball in any forward direction (**B**), then runs to the post and touches it. She next has to run back behind the starting line without being caught on the way. ▶ The fielders can only catch the runner by throwing the ball and hitting her with it below the knee (**C**). ▶ Any hits elsewhere do not count. Fielders must not touch the runner in any other way, nor must the ball be kicked by anyone. ▶ A fielder must stand still when she is holding the ball.

The runner aims to get back to the starting line without being touched by the ball.

The fielder who succeeds in touching the runner below the knee with the ball becomes the next runner.

TIG

Number This can be played by four or more of any age who are fit enough to run until exhausted.

Place and time Play this game outdoors in a large space such as a field or beach. The playing area should be clearly defined before the game starts. It can be played any time and in any weather.

Equipment None.

How to play ▶ One player begins as the chaser (**A**). The others have to run away to avoid being touched by him (**B**). He has to chase the players and try to touch, or

'tig', one (**C**). ▶ The player who has been tigged is then the chaser (**D**) and chases the other players. The new chaser is not allowed to tig the one who has just been chaser immediately, but may tig him after chasing other players. ▶ The chaser is not allowed to keep chasing the same person, and nobody is allowed to have a rest. The aim is to remain in the game for as long as possible and to be tigged the least number of times. There is usually no outright winner as this game goes on and on until everyone is exhausted.

SHIPWRECKS

Number The game is for four or more of any age who are fit enough to run until exhausted.

Place and time It can be played any time outdoors where there are several objects on which players can climb to avoid stepping on the ground – for example, on a beach where rocks protrude from the sand or in a field where there are climbable trees or mounds.

Young children could play this indoors by jumping onto cushions scattered on the floor.

Another good location is a children's adventure playground where there are swings, roundabouts, climbing frames and slides.

If there is no adventure playground, any space can be used by agreeing a number of 'safe places' such as drain covers, rocks, bushes or a lamppost, and marking

other safe places as small islands on the ground. The rest of the ground is counted as 'sea'.

Equipment None.

How to play ▶ One person is chosen as the pirate (**A**) and has to chase the others. The ground is the sea and the players can find a safe haven by keeping their feet out of the water (**B**). ▶ If the pirate touches a player (**C**) while she has even one foot in the sea, that player becomes the new pirate (**D**). ▶ The pirate is not allowed to keep chasing the same person. ▶ Nobody is allowed to have a rest. ▶ Nobody is allowed to stay in a safe spot for longer than it takes to count to 10. ▶ Only one person may occupy a safe spot at any one time. There is usually no outright winner as this game goes on and on until everyone is exhausted.

THREE LIVES

Number Any number of any age can play.

Place and time It is played indoors or outdoors where there is space to run around and throw a soft ball. It can be played at any time of the year in any weather.

Equipment One large, soft ball is needed.

How to play ▶ Everyone begins the game with three 'lives'. The ball is placed on the ground and the players

take their positions (**A**). The ball is now picked up and thrown by whoever is nearest to it (**B**). The thrower aims at another person. ▶ Whoever catches the ball can have a throw, aiming to hit another player. ▶ When a player is hit below the thigh, he loses a life (**C**). But the game continues (**D**), and whoever picks up the ball now aims it at another player. Players who lose all three lives must drop out. The last player left in the game wins.

CHAIR CARRY
Number This game is for teams of three. Any age can play but the game is best for players of similar strengths and sizes.
Place and time It can be played indoors in a large room or anywhere outdoors in fine weather.
Equipment None.
Preparation A playing area is marked out, with a starting line and a finishing line, using books, leaves or piles of coats.
How to play ▶ Each team forms a threesome (**A**). Two members of each team make a chair with their

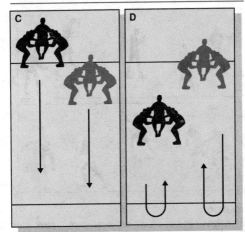

hands and lift up the third member (**B**). They then carry
her to the end of the room or playing area (**C**) and back
(**D**). ▶ Then a different team member is carried and so
on until every team member has been carried out and
back.

Variation This game can also be adapted for playing
in a shallow swimming pool where the players can walk
in the water.

Swimmers would enjoy playing this game by pulling
each other through the water as they float.

The first team to complete carrying each member is the
winning team.

TABOO

Number The game is for four or more of any age who are able to run.

Place and time It is suitable for outdoors in a large space such as a field or beach. The playing area must be clearly defined before the game starts by marking out an area with stones or piles of coats. The game can be played at any time and in any weather.

Equipment None.

How to play ▶ Players take up positions prepared to run (**A**). One player is chosen to be 'it' (perhaps the player whose first name begins with a letter nearest to the beginning of the alphabet), and begins by chasing the others. When he touches a player (**B**), he shouts 'Taboo', thus passing on an imaginary taboo. ▶ The

player who has been touched must put his hand on the taboo spot where he was touched as he chases someone else. ▶ Only when he touches another player (**C**) does he lose the taboo. ▶ Players should try to touch each other in the most disabling spot; for example, if touched on the foot, a player will have to hop about, holding his foot (**D**). ▶ The one who has just passed the taboo on to a new player cannot be touched by that player. ▶ The player with the taboo is not allowed to keep chasing the same person. ▶ Nobody is allowed to drop out and then return. ▶ If a player is so disabled by the taboo that he cannot get near enough to another player to pass on the taboo, he must drop out and nominate a new chaser. The aim is to be the last one still in the game.

TOUCH COLOUR

Number The game is for any number, of any age, fit enough to run.

Place and time The game can be played outdoors in a fairly large space such as a field, beach or playground. The playing area should be clearly defined, by using coats or stones to mark out the space before the game starts. It can be played any time in fine weather.

Equipment None.

How to play ▶ One player begins as the chaser by standing in the middle of a circle formed by the other players (**A**). She calls out a particular colour. ▶ Players who are visibly wearing the colour or who can run and touch the colour anywhere in the defined area become immune. ▶ The chaser has to chase the players (**B**) and

touch someone who is not immune (**C**). ▶ The player
who is touched first is then the new chaser and chooses
a new colour (**D**). ▶ No chaser is allowed to keep
chasing the same person. ▶ Nobody is allowed to have
a rest. ▶ It is the chaser's right to decide if a colour is
exactly what she called; for example, if a deep pink can
count as red or if a shade of blue can count as sea-green.
▶ Players may touch the colour on objects or people.
▶ After the players have run out of single colours to
call, the chaser may call colour combinations, such as
red and brown, or green, blue and yellow; or patterns
such as red dots, pink and grey stripes, or flowery
designs in green, red and yellow. There is usually no
outright winner as this game continues until everyone is
exhausted.

BUDGE

Number This is a game for eight or more of any age who can run around energetically. There must be an even number of players.

Place and time It is played outdoors in a field, on a beach or in a playground. The playing area is clearly defined by placing coats or stones around the space before the game starts.

Equipment None.

How to play ▶ Each player chooses a partner and each couple stands, one behind the other, in a circle (**A**). There should be an equal distance between each couple. ▶ One couple is chosen to begin. The person in front becomes the chaser and the person behind, the runner (**B**). ▶ As the runner is being chased, he can

dodge around the other pairs and move beyond the circle within the agreed play area. ▶ When he slips in front of another couple (**C**), he is safe and the person at the back of that couple then becomes the new runner. ▶ As a runner stands in front of a couple, he shouts 'Budge' to make sure the person at the back moves away. ▶ If the chaser touches the runner, they immediately change roles (**D**). ▶ Throughout the game, there are only two people running at any one time; but in a good game, the players are changing places very quickly. The players aim to avoid being touched. There is no outright winner. Players usually continue until they are exhausted.

SHADOW TOUCH

Number The game is for any number of any age who can run energetically.

Place and time It is played outdoors. Sunshine is essential.

Equipment None.

How to play ▶ The limits of the play area must be agreed, but it should not be too large if there are only three or four players. ▶ This is basically a game of Tig, where one person chases the other players (**A**),

attempting to touch one of them. However, the chaser must touch a player's shadow (**B**). The chaser can touch the shadow with a hand or a foot. ▶ When this happens, the player whose shadow is touched becomes the new chaser (**C**). ▶ The only way a player can find a 'safe haven' is to hide in the shadow of, for example, a tree or a wall (**D**). Otherwise players must keep running to avoid their shadows being touched. The aim is to stay in the game without having to drop out exhausted.

CROSS TOUCH

Number The game is for five or more of any age who can run energetically.

Place and time It is best played outdoors in good weather. A reasonable space is required and the area within which the game will be played should be marked out before the game starts.

Equipment None.

How to play ▶ One player is chosen to be 'it' and chases the others (**A**), trying to touch one of them.

When he succeeds in doing so (**B**), the person touched
becomes the new chaser. ▶ However, the game has a
variation which makes it particularly lively. When the
distance between the chaser and the person being chased
is wide enough, another player can cross between them
(**C**). The chaser must then pursue the player who
crossed his path (**D**). The aim is to stay in the game
without dropping out exhausted.

POISON

Number The game needs four to eleven players, who can be of any age.

Place and time It can be played outdoors at any time in good weather. The area within which the game will be played should be marked out beforehand.

Equipment None.

How to play ▶ One player is chosen as the caller and stands with her arms crossed and her hands outstretched. Each player takes hold of one of the caller's fingers, very lightly, but must not lose contact – though standing as far away from the caller as possible (**A**). ▶ The caller begins the game by saying, for example, 'I went to a shop and bought a bottle of lemonade.' ▶ The caller then repeats her statement, each time with a different thing she bought, such as

sweets, a packet of hankies, some potatoes . . . and so on. Sometimes she might stutter on one of the letters, saying 'p- p- p- pepper'. ▶ The caller's aim is to keep the players at the ready for when she says 'I went to the shop and bought a bottle of POISON.' (**B**). At this point, the players all run and the caller chases them, aiming to touch one of them. If she does so, the touched player becomes the new caller. ▶ The new caller then stands in the centre of the play area with arms crossed and hands outstretched, and the item-calling ritual starts again. ▶ Any player who loses contact before the word 'poison' is said must immediately take the place of the caller. ▶ Anyone who twice loses contact too soon is out of the game. The aim is to be the last person in the game.

BLIND MAN'S BUFF

Number Four or more players of any age can play.

Place and time It can be played indoors in a room or outdoors in a small area not much bigger than a room. The playing area should be agreed and marked out before the game starts.

Equipment One scarf is needed for use as a blindfold.

How to play ▶ The first chaser is chosen, stands in the middle of the space and is blindfolded (**A**). He is then turned round on the spot a few times to disorientate him (**B**). ▶ The chaser then has to try to

find and touch one of the other players. ▶ The players try to confuse him by swooping around him and making noises (**C**). ▶ When the chaser touches a player, that player must stand still (**D**). ▶ In the outdoor game, the one who is caught is then blindfolded and becomes the chaser. ▶ In the indoor game, the chaser has to identify the person he has caught by touching her face. If he guesses right, he can hand over his blindfold to the new chaser. If not, he has to continue the chase until he catches someone he *can* identify. The aim of the game is to avoid being caught.

JINGLE BELLS

Number This game is for four or more players of similar age. Young children should not be mixed with older children for this game.

Place and time It is played indoors in a large room or outdoors in a space about twice the size of an average room. The area within which the game will be played should be marked out and be free from any hazards, such as furniture, trees or passing cars. A non-player would be useful to ensure players do not wander too far.

Equipment A blindfold for each player, such as a

scarf or large handkerchief, is required.

How to play ▶ One player is chosen to be the quarry, and will be chased by all the other players. All the chasing players put on a blindfold. They then try to catch the quarry, who can run about where she likes, dodging to avoid her pursuers (**A**). But she must not go outside the play area. ▶ The quarry should make a sound like a bell every now and then by singing 'tinkle, tinkle, ring, ring,' and so on (**B**). This is to guide the chasers. ▶ The chaser who catches the quarry changes place with the quarry (**C**), and the game continues (**D**). This is an ongoing game with no outright winner.

MR WOLF

Number The game is for four or more players of any age.

Place and time It is played any time outdoors.

Equipment None.

Preparation A starting line should be scratched on the ground with chalk. Otherwise, a fence or a row of rocks can mark the starting line.

How to play ▶ One player is chosen to be Mr Wolf. He walks slowly away from the starting line with all the other players following behind him – as close to him as they dare to get (**A**). ▶ One by one, they ask him the time by saying, 'What time is it, Mr Wolf?' ▶ Without

turning round, Mr Wolf replies to each question with any time he chooses at random – for example, 6 o'clock, 23 minutes to 9, 3 o'clock, bedtime, 4 o'clock, and so on (**B**). ▶ When Mr Wolf replies, 'Dinner time!', everyone must run back to the safety of the starting line (**C**). ▶ The one Mr Wolf catches, by touching, becomes the new Mr Wolf (**D**). ▶ If someone starts to run back before Mr Wolf says 'Dinner time', that player has to stand closest behind Mr Wolf. The point of the game is to enjoy the sheer tension of not knowing when the chase will begin. The game continues until everyone wants to stop.

RUNNING ACROSS

Number The game needs an odd number of players –
at least nine – who should be very energetic. They can
be of any age.

Place and time It can be played outdoors at any
time in a large square space. The playing area should be
marked out using leaves, stones or piles of coats.

Equipment None.

How to play ▶ One player is the chaser and stands
in the middle of the play space. The others form two
equal teams, standing facing each other in lines on two

opposite sides of the playing area (**A**). ▶ The game starts when both teams rush across the playing area to the opposite side, passing the other team on the way. ▶ During their scramble, the chaser tries to catch as many players as possible by touching them (**B**). Any player who is touched stays in the middle and becomes a chaser, too (**C**). ▶ The two teams then dash across again, trying to avoid being caught by the two chasers (**D**). ▶ The game continues in this way until all except one player have been caught and made a chaser. This last one is the winner.

CHINESE WALL

Number This is for four or more energetic players of any age.

Place and time The game is ideally played on a firm sandy beach, since two lines have to be marked on the ground. But as only a moderate amount of space is needed, Chinese Wall can also be played in a garden on the grass.

Equipment None.

Preparation Two parallel lines, about one metre apart, are drawn on the ground. The lines should be about six metres long if there are four players and extended by a metre for every extra player.

The width of the playing area is limited by the length of the lines.

The space between the lines represents the position of the Chinese Wall.

How to play ▶ One person is chosen to be the catcher and stands between the lines (**A**). ▶ The other players are the runners and stand behind one of the lines, facing the catcher. ▶ The catcher calls 'Go' and everyone has to get across the wall without being

caught by the catcher. ▶ If the catcher touches a runner (**B**), the two players exchange places. ▶ The catcher must have both feet within the lines of the wall when she touches a runner, but the runner's feet do not have to be on the wall. ▶ When all runners are across, the command 'Go' is shouted again and players have to run back across the wall. The aim is to run to and fro across the wall without ever being caught.

Variations

– A non-player can be asked to call 'Go', or the command can be called several times in quick succession, creating a lot of furious running. There can then be a pause. The 'Go' command can also be made loudly or softly to catch the players unawares. These are particularly good ways to add tension to the game.

– If there are at least six players, two catchers can stand on the wall.

– The runners who are caught can join the catchers until there is only one runner left. In this case, the aim is to be the last runner left in the game, who is declared the winner.

FARMER FARMER

Number Four or more of any age can play this game. It is especially popular with younger children.

Place and time It can be played outdoors in fine weather.

Equipment None.

Preparation Two parallel lines are marked on the ground of a playing area, using chalk or string. These lines represent the banks of a river.

How to play ▶ One person is chosen to be the farmer, who stands in the middle of the river (**A**). The others all stand facing her on one bank of the river. ▶

Any player calls out, 'Farmer, farmer, may we cross your golden river?' ▶ The farmer replies, 'Yes if you have . . .' and states either a colour they must be wearing or an object they must be carrying or can pick up to carry across to the opposite side. ▶ Those who conform to the instructions can walk across the river without hindrance. ▶ Those who do not conform must run across (**B**), trying to avoid being touched by the farmer (**C**). ▶ Anyone who is caught is out of the game, and the game continues (**D**). The aim is to win by being the last person in the game. The winner becomes the farmer in the next game.

WALK THE PLANK

Number This can be played by five or more players of similar ages. It would be a good idea to have an adult close by to keep an eye on things.

Place and time It can be played anywhere outdoors on a soft surface where two parallel lines can be marked about three metres apart. This game can also be fun if played on a safe beach where the edge of the sea counts as one of the lines. In this case, players need to have bare feet as they will dash in and out of the water. It is best played during warm weather.

Equipment None.

How to play ▶ One person is chosen as the captain and stands between the lines (**A**). The players face him, standing behind one of the lines. ▶ The captain challenges one of the players, saying, 'Join the crew or walk the plank?' ▶ If the player replies, 'Join the

crew,' he goes into the middle and stands by the captain (**B**). ▶ If he replies, 'Walk the plank,' he immediately starts running for the opposite side and the captain tries to catch him. ▶ If he gets caught, he is persuaded to join the crew. This is done by 'torturing' him until he agrees to join. 'Torturing' should be playful – tickling the player, for example. Once persuaded, the player joins the crew and helps the captain to catch and persuade other players challenged by the captain. ▶ If the player crosses without being caught, he shouts, 'Overboard!' Everyone else must then rush across to join him. Nobody tries to catch them (**C**). ▶ The captain then challenges another player (**D**).

The aim is to win by being the only player who has not joined the crew. The winner then becomes captain for the next round.

KINGS, QUEENS, JACKS

Number The game is for four or more energetic players of any age.

Place and time It is played outdoors where there is reasonable running space. The game may be played at any time in fine weather.

Equipment None.

Preparation A roughly circular running space must be clearly defined on the ground, using chalk or long ropes. It should measure about 7–10 metres in diameter. Everything outside the circle is considered to be in the safe area.

How to play ▶ One person, known as the caller, stands in the centre of the circle. ▶ All the other players stand anywhere in the safe area outside the circle. ▶ The caller can choose to shout one of three things: Kings, Queens or Jacks. ▶ If she calls 'Kings',

every player has to run straight across to safe ground on the other side of the circle (**A**) without being caught by the caller and put in the middle of the circle. ▶ If she calls 'Queens', everyone has to hop across without being knocked over by the caller, who is also hopping. Anyone knocked over has to join the caller in the middle of the circle. ▶ If she calls 'Jacks', any player who moves a muscle is out and has to sit down in the safe area. ▶ The caller then makes another call and those who joined her now help to catch running or hopping players (**B**). ▶ The game can become very exciting if the caller makes calls in quick succession and does some feinting and dodging to confuse the players. The aim of the game is to win by being the one remaining player. The winner then becomes the caller for the next game.

MANHUNT

Number This game is for four or more players of any age.

Place and time It is played outdoors in a place where there are many natural features which could be used as hiding places.

Equipment None.

How to play ▶ One person is chosen as the hunted, the other players being the hunters. ▶ A home base is chosen, such as a particular rock, wall, lamppost, pile of pebbles or circle drawn in sand. ▶ The hunters then crowd round the home base, close their eyes and start counting up to 100. One person should count out loud so that the hunted player can hear while he goes to find a hiding place (**A**). ▶ When the count is completed, the hunters begin the manhunt. Hunters may not gather round the home base waiting for their quarry; they must stay at least three metres away from it during the hunt, and they must actively hunt for the hunted. ▶ To avoid being caught, the hunted can change his hiding place as

often as he likes. His aim is to get back to the safety of the home base without being caught by any of the hunters. The hunted is safe once he touches or stands on the home base. ▶ The hunted is caught when he is seen by any of the hunters, and has to come out of hiding to be taken back to the home base. If he does not, he is out of the game. ▶ The hunter who first sees the hunted becomes the next one to be hunted. ▶ If the hunted gets back to the home base undetected (**B**), he nominates the next player to be hunted. ▶ The game is especially exciting when the hunted invents tactics to distract or confuse the hunters, such as throwing a stick to make it sound as if he is somewhere else in the vicinity.

Every hunted player who reaches the home base without being caught is given three cheers or some other agreed reward.

The aim of the hunters is to catch the hunted before he gets back to the home base, so cooperation between hunters is a good idea.

BLOCKY HIDE AND SEEK

Number The game is for four or more energetic players of any age.

Place and time It is suitable for outdoors where there are natural features to provide hiding places. This game can be played during the day, though some older children may enjoy it better on a summer's evening.

Equipment If a scarf is available, it can be used as a blindfold, but it is not necessary.

How to play ▶ A home base is chosen, such as a post or rock. This is known as the 'block'. ▶ One person is chosen to be the blocker. She stands by the block and either shuts her eyes or blindfolds herself with a scarf. She then counts out loud in ones, up to an agreed number; 100 is usually suitable. ▶ While she counts, all the other players run and find hiding places (**A**). They each try to keep the block in view because their aim is to get back to the block without being seen by the blocker. ▶ When the blocker has finished counting, she leaves the scarf (if one is used) at the block, and goes off to find the hidden players. ▶ These

hiders stay still in their hiding places until the blocker
finishes counting. Then they can move anywhere as
they try to get to the block without being seen (**B**). ▶ A
player who gets back to the block, touches it and shouts,
'One, two, three, block home,' is free and safe from the
blocker. ▶ However, if the blocker sees one of the
players, she must then try to block him by running back
to touch the block herself, shouting, 'One, two, three, I
spy . . .', ending with the name of the person seen. ▶ A
player who is blocked in this way is out of the game and
must leave his hiding place and stay near the block. ▶
A player who is seen by the blocker can, of course, try
to race the blocker back to the block and free himself by
touching it first. ▶ When all the players have been
freed or blocked, the first person who was blocked, or
caught out, becomes the next blocker and the game
begins again.
The game generally continues until everyone is tired
and agrees to stop.

SARDINES

Number At least four players of any age can play.
Place and time It can be played outdoors, in fine weather, where there are a number of natural hiding places. Sardines is also a popular game indoors during dark evenings.
Equipment None.
How to play ▶ One player goes to hide (**A**) while the remaining players stay together and count up to 100. ▶ The player hiding must try to get into a hiding place where there will be enough space for others to join him. ▶ When the count is completed, the seekers

all go looking independently for the one who is hidden (**B**). If a player finds the hiding place, he does not tell anyone. Instead, he quietly joins the first player, and they both stay hidden together (**C**). ▶ Everyone tries to find the hiding place and get into it, making a 'tin of sardines'. The last person to find the sardines is the loser (**D**) and is usually chased back to the starting point. Sometimes, if players have been squashed into a small hiding area, they may be too stiff to give chase! ▶ The loser then becomes the next player to go and hide, while the others begin counting again.

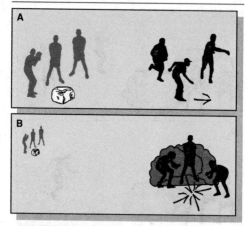

TRACKING

Number The game is for four to eight players in two teams. Any age can enjoy this game, but younger children should be mixed in a team with older ones.

Place and time It is best played in dry weather in a large park.

Equipment Players should collect small stones or twigs to use. A starting point is marked with a large rock or a pile of leaves.

How to play ▶ The players divide into two teams. One team waits, with eyes closed, at the starting point for about five minutes. ▶ The other team goes off to lay a track of arrows at intervals of 9–12 metres (**A**).

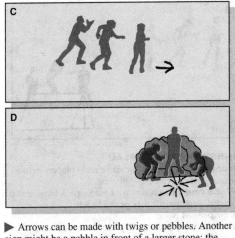

▶ Arrows can be made with twigs or pebbles. Another sign might be a pebble in front of a larger stone; the smaller points the direction to go. ▶ The first team eventually has to find a hiding place, known as 'home', which is usually indicated with four closely placed arrows pointing inwards to each other (**B**). ▶ The second team has to find the home by following the tracks laid by the first team (**C**). As they find the arrows, these are destroyed to avoid confusion in the next game. ▶ When home has been found, the teams change places – trackers become hiders and vice versa (**D**). ▶ Tracking begins from the last home base.

HOIST THE GREEN FLAG

Number This game is for six or more players in two teams. Any age can enjoy playing.

Place and time It is played outdoors. A large area is needed, perhaps in a park or at a beach.

Equipment None.

How to play ▶ Players gather at a spot that they agree to call the 'den'. It could be a tent on a camping holiday, a rock on the beach or a particular bush or tree. ▶ Two players are chosen to be leaders. The leaders select their teams and agree which team shall be hiders and which seekers. ▶ The seekers stay at the den with their eyes closed while the hiders are led away by their leader, to take an indirect route to a hiding place (**A**). ▶ The leader of the hiding team then returns to the den and either describes the route verbally or draws it on the ground, if there is soft earth or sand. ▶ The description might be like this:

– ten paces to an oak tree, then turn a corner;

– take 14 paces round a flowerbed;
– take 23 paces past water, then pass under an arch;
– go through a gate and walk 40 paces over a small hill past three cottages;
– then you will come to our hiding place.

The leader of the hiders then goes back to the hiding place, usually in the wrong direction to mislead the seekers. ▶ The seekers then follow their leader, trying to find the hiding place from the description given. Their leader gives instructions along the way. ▶ When they see a member of the hiding team, the leader shouts 'Spotted!' and tells his team to run for the den. ▶ If the hiders are about to be seen or the seekers are far off-track, the leader of the hiding team can shout to her team to 'Run for the den!' ▶ The leader of the first team back to the den, raises her arms and shouts, 'Hoist the green flag' (**B**). ▶ The first team back to the den are the winners and become the hiders for the next round of the game.

HUNT THE KEG

Number At least six players of any age can take part in two teams.

Place and time It is played outdoors in good weather. A large park in a town or the countryside, or a beach, are ideal places to play this game.

Equipment Any small item is needed. This can be an object in someone's pocket – for example, an unopened packet of chewing gum, a penknife, a badge – or a small pebble or twig. This small item is called the 'keg'.

Preparation The teams agree on a den, which could be marked by a rock, a tree, or someone's coat folded on the ground.

A feature nearby, such as a bush, is chosen to represent the coastguard station.

How to play ▶ Players divide into two teams – the smugglers and the coastguards. ▶ One of the smugglers carries the keg in his hand all through the game, but nobody in the other team must know who this is. ▶ The coastguards stay by the den (**A**), counting up to 100 and keeping their eyes closed, while

the smugglers scatter and hide, each in a different place.
▶ When the count is completed, the coastguards begin searching for the smugglers, while the smugglers try to reach the den without being caught. ▶ If a smuggler is caught or even seen, the coastguard challenges him by shouting, 'Deliver the keg' (**B**). ▶ If the smuggler does not have it, he is taken prisoner and has to stay at the coastguard station. ▶ If the smuggler has the keg, he must give it up and the game ends.

The aim of the game is for the smuggler with the keg to get to the den. The coastguards must try to capture the smuggler with the keg. If the smugglers manage to get the keg back to the den, that team remains as smugglers for the next game. Otherwise, for the next game, the smugglers and coastguards change places.

Tactics This game offers an opportunity for team members to cooperate in achieving their ends. For example, smugglers can allow themselves to be caught to distract the coastguards from seeing the player with the keg.

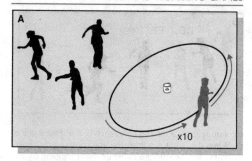

TIN CAN TOMMY

Number The game is for four or more energetic players of any age.

Place and time It is suitable for playing outdoors where players have plenty of space and places in which to hide. It is best played in dry weather.

Equipment A used drinks can or other empty tin is needed. Alternatively, a beach ball could be used.

How to play ▶ A circle is marked on the ground with chalk or string, or drawn in the sand, and the can (or ball) is placed inside it. One player is chosen to be the canner or seeker. The other players are the hiders.

▶ To start the game, the can is kicked (or the ball is thrown) along the ground by one of the hiders. The canner has to go after it, pick it up and walk backwards to replace it in the circle. She then must walk ten times round the circle (**A**). ▶ Meanwhile, the hiders all run off in different directions to hide, where they stay, still and quiet. ▶ When the canner has completed the ritual,

she may go and look for the hiders. ▶ When she sees a
hider, she dashes back to the circle, puts her foot on the
tin can or ball and shouts, 'Tin Can Tommy, one, two,
three . . . . Is who I see ——?', calling the name of the
hider she has seen (**B**). ▶ The hider who is caught this
way must go and stand captive near the circle. ▶ The
canner continues to seek other hiders, and capture them.
However, when she is not looking, one of the hiders can
run to the circle, kick the can or ball out of it, and
thereby release the captured hider, who runs away to
hide again. ▶ If the canner calls the wrong name,
everyone comes out of hiding and the game starts again
with the same person as canner. ▶ Any captured hider
is now freed. But anyone who has been freed three
times cannot be set free again.

The aim of the game is for the canner to capture all the
hiders, while the hiders must try to avoid being caught.
The game ends when all the hiders are caught. The first
one to be captured is the canner for the next game.

CAT AND MOUSE
Number At least ten young children who enjoy a rough and tumble can play.
Place and time It is played on a soft surface outdoors, in dry weather.
Equipment None.
How to play ▶ One person is chosen to be the cat and another, the mouse. ▶ All the other players grasp hands and form a circle. Those forming the circle are on the side of the mouse, who stands inside the circle

(**A**). ▶ The cat, who is outside the circle, tries to get inside it to catch the mouse. The players in the circle have to push together to stop him. ▶ If the cat breaks through into the circle, they must let the mouse out to run around (**B**). ▶ If the cat catches the mouse, the mouse must lie on the floor, as if dead, while the cat pretends to eat it. ▶ If the cat fails to catch the mouse after an agreed time, the cat loses and the mouse has won. ▶ A new cat and mouse are then chosen for the next game.

2. Throwing and aiming games

WATER BALLOON
Number Any number can play in pairs (minimum two pairs).
Place and time The game is played outdoors where water from a tap is available. It is best in warm weather.
Equipment One balloon per pair of players is filled with water and tied. Extra water-filled balloons are needed.
How to play ▶ The two players of each pair stand facing each other (**A**), one holding the water balloon.

On the word 'Go', the balloon is thrown to the partner, who throws it back, and so on. After each throw is made, the thrower takes one step backwards (**B**). When a balloon is dropped or bursts, that game ends (**C**). ▶ Players aim to have the greatest distance between them without dropping or bursting the balloon when it is thrown.

Variation The game can be varied by having a time limit and introducing two or three rounds to the competition.

SQUIRT THE CORK

Number The game is for four or more players divided into two equal teams.

Place and time It is played outdoors, during dry weather.

Equipment Each team needs a cork of equal size (such as a wine bottle cork) and two plastic washing-up liquid bottles, suitable for squirting.

Preparation Both of each team's bottles should be filled with water, one for use and one to replace it when empty. The corks are placed on a starting line. A finishing line is drawn about 5 metres away.

How to play ▶ Two players – one member of each team – start (**A**) by squirting water at their team's cork

to move it along the ground (**B**). ▶ When a player has pushed the cork to the finishing line, she picks it up and runs back to the starting line (**C**). Then the second player of that team squirts the cork, and so on (**D**). The empty bottle can be refilled while the other one is in use, so there is a constant supply of water. ▶ The first team in which each player has squirted the cork to the finishing line wins.

Variation A lightweight ball, such as a ping pong ball, can be used instead of a cork. If only one bottle is used, participants will have to stop play while it is refilled. This can add to the excitement of the game, especially when it is played on a beach and players must run to the sea to fill the bottle.

HOT BALLOONS

Number Eight or more players of any age can play.

Place and time It is played outdoors, especially in a large field, garden or on the beach. Water must be available. Any time of the year is suitable, provided players don't mind getting wet.

Equipment Five or six balloons are used, half-filled with water and tied. Two are kept in play at one time, and the others are put aside as spares.

How to play ▶ One person is chosen as the leader. The other players make a circle around the leader and spread out as far as they can go while still touching fingertips. ▶ The leader has two balloons. One is thrown to any player at random who then has to throw

it to the neighbour on the left (**A**). This balloon continues to be thrown clockwise round the circle from player to player. ▶ Meanwhile, the leader throws the other balloon to any player in the circle who has to throw it back. The leader then throws this balloon to the next person, in clockwise order, who returns it and so on (**B**).
▶ If a player drops or bursts the balloon, he is out and sits down, staying in that position in the circle so the balloon may have to be thrown over him. ▶ If a balloon bursts, the leader goes and gets a spare balloon.
▶ Each player tries to be the last player left standing. The winner then becomes the leader for the next game.

BUNGLE BUNGLE

Number The game is for any number of players from three upwards.

Place and time It is suitable for outdoors in a large, flat area, such as a playing field or a sandy beach, at any time of the year.

Equipment One balloon partly filled with water and a metre length of string are needed per player. The balloons should be blown up fully after being partly filled with water.

Preparation Each player ties her balloon to the string, and the string to one wrist, leaving about half-a-metre between wrist and balloon.

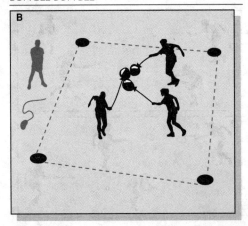

A playing area is marked out on the sand. On a field, the corners of a playing square can be marked with sticks or coats. Allow about 4 square metres per player when deciding how big to make the playing area.

How to play ▶ By swinging their balloons at others' balloons, players try to burst as many balloons as possible while protecting their own (**A**). When a player's balloon is burst, he is out and stands outside the playing area (**B**). ▶ Players aim to be the last person with an unburst balloon.

Variation Players could each have two balloons, one tied to each wrist, and stay in the game until both balloons are burst.

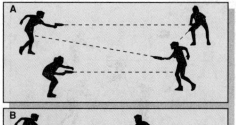

TATTOO

Number This is a messy game and can be played by any number from two upwards. Players can be of any age. Everyone should wear old bathing costumes. Little children probably would be best wearing nothing.

Place and time It is played outdoors in warm weather where water is available.

Equipment One squeeze bottle, such as a washing-up liquid bottle, is needed per player, and some water-based poster paints.

Preparation Players paint tattoos on themselves before the game begins. Tattoos can be words, a picture, or just a pattern, and they should be painted on

any bare skin on the chest, tummy, arms and legs but not on faces. The number of tattoos painted should be agreed in advance – for example, one on each arm – so that each player has the same number. The squeeze bottles are filled with water.

How to play ▶ Everyone has one bottle of water to squirt at the others, trying to smudge their paint while protecting his own (**A**). ▶ Players drop out as the water is used up in their squeeze bottles (**B** and **C**). ▶ The game ends when all players have used up the water in their squeeze bottles (**D**). ▶ Each player tries to be the one who manages to keep at least one of his tattoos unsmudged.

POP IT

Number Any number can play in two or more equal teams. Help from an adult will be needed for making points on the sticks and for tying the rope above the players' heads. It is not a suitable game for small children.

Place and time It is played outdoors where two trees or poles are available, about 5 metres apart.

Equipment The game requires a rope about 7 metres long; a dozen balloons; a dozen pieces of string about half-a-metre long; and a stick, 1 metre long, for each team. The stick should be whittled to a point at one end. Players should be careful not to point the sharp end of the stick at other players, and not to stand in the playing area while the game is played.

Preparation The rope is tied above head height between the two trees or poles. The balloons are half-filled with water. They are tied to the rope and left hanging from the strings. A playing line is drawn about a metre in front of the rope.

How to play ▶ The teams sit well back from the playing line. The first player from each team stands on the playing line, holding a stick (**A**). When the game begins, they try to burst any balloon using the stick. When a player has burst a balloon, she runs back to her team and passes the stick to the next player, who runs to the playing line and tries to burst another balloon (**B**).

▶ Players try to be the team that bursts the most balloons.

CATCH A SPONGE

Number Any even number can play in two equal teams. Players should wear bathing costumes.

Place and time It can be played anywhere outdoors in warm weather.

Equipment A large plastic bucket full of water, two plastic bowls of equal size and a large supply of small sponges are needed.

Preparation Two parallel playing lines are drawn on the ground about 2 metres apart. Each team stands on a line, facing each other. One member of each team, the catcher, stands with the opposing team, holding his team's plastic bowl.

A large number of sponges should be left soaking in the large bucket of water at one end of the play area, halfway between the two lines.

How to play ▶ On the word 'Go', players in turn collect a sponge, return behind their playing line and attempt to throw wet sponges into their team's bowl opposite. No physical contact is allowed (**A**). ▶ The catcher stands in one place but can move the bowl back and forth to try to catch the sponges (**B**). Players can throw sponges at opposing players to distract them.

▶ Each team tries to catch the greatest number of sponges, which can be collected in a pile behind the catcher.

BEHIND THE CURTAIN

Number Any number in two equal teams can play.

Place and time It is played outdoors in dry weather, if water is used, or indoors in a large hall, if soft balls are to be used.

Equipment The game requires several balloons half-filled with water, or several large, soft or lightweight balls. A washing line or length of rope is also needed, strung between two poles or trees about 3 metres from the ground, and a large old bedsheet or plastic sheet.

Preparation The sheet is draped over the line or

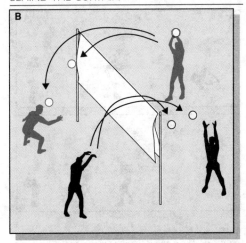

rope, with space underneath it. The teams stand either side of the line.

How to play ▶ *With water balloons.* Players throw two balloons back and forth over the line. Anyone who drops or bursts a balloon scores a penalty point for his team (**A**). When a balloon is dropped, another is put into play to replace it. ▶ *With soft balls.* Players throw two or three balls at a time back and forth over the sheet. Every dropped ball scores a penalty point (**B**). ▶ At the end of a given time limit, the team with the least number of penalty points wins.

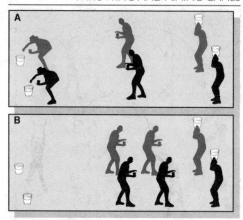

BUCKET HEAD

Number The game is for any number in two equal teams, wearing bathing costumes or old clothes. The leader, in particular, will get wet.

Place and time It is played outdoors in warm weather.

Equipment Two buckets of water are placed on the ground. The game also requires two other lightweight plastic buckets or containers of equal size, 40 clothes pegs in two different colours, and a plastic cup for each team member.

Preparation Using both hands, the leader of each team holds a small, empty bucket, open side up, on her

head. Pegged to each leader's clothes are 20 clothes pegs in one colour.

The large buckets of water and plastic cups, for each team, are placed out of the way of the playing area, but accessible.

How to play ▶ On the word 'Go', teams fill their plastic cups with water (**A**) and pour them into their leader's bucket (**B** and **C**). Once they have done that, team members also have to pluck the pegs from the leader of the opposing team (**D**). ▶ When both teams have each collected their 20 pegs, the game ends. Players try to be the team with the most water in its leader's bucket at the end of the game.

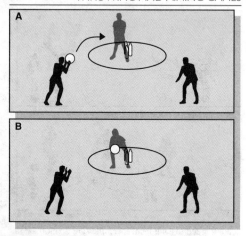

POLYBOTTLES

Number The game is for two or more players.

Place and time It is played outdoors at any time or in a hall indoors.

Equipment The game requires three plastic bottles with screw tops, about one-third full of water; a large beach ball or other lightweight ball; and a piece of chalk or a rope to mark out a circle.

Preparation A circle about 2 metres in diameter is marked out. One player stands the three bottles in the centre and stays in the circle to defend them. All the other players spread out round the outside of the circle.

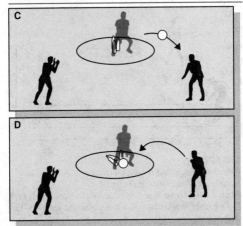

How to play ▶ The ball is thrown at the bottles in attempts to knock them down (**A**). The defender tries to prevent this happening by intercepting the ball (**B**). After catching the ball, the defender throws it back to any player (**C**). ▶ If a bottle is knocked over, the defender stands it up again (**D**). Otherwise he is not allowed to touch the bottles. ▶ The aim is to knock down all three bottles before the defender can replace them. The person who achieves this becomes the new defender.

SKITTLES

Number The game is for two or more players of any age, divided into two equal teams.

Place and time It is played indoors or outdoors, in dry weather, where there is a flat surface at least 10–12 metres long.

Equipment Ten plastic bottles or ten cardboard tubes numbered one to ten are used. These are the skittles. Six soft balls, such as tennis balls, will also be needed, three for each team. Paper and pencil are needed for scoring.

Preparation A skittle alley, about 1½ metres wide and at least 10 metres long, could be marked with chalk or two ropes. A starting line should be clearly marked, as should a cross for the positioning of the ten skittles in a group at the other end of the alley.

How to play ▶ The first player rolls the three balls down the alley, one at a time, aiming to knock down as many skittles as possible (**A**). One player writes down

the numbers of any skittles knocked down (**B**). The
balls are collected after each turn and given to the next
team member. ▶ All skittles are returned to their
standing positions, and the first player in the opposing
team then rolls his three balls. Any skittles knocked
down are again recorded. ▶ Players take turns rolling
their three balls and scoring, for their team, the numbers
marked on the skittles they knock down. ▶ Bowling
continues until all players in each team have had a turn.
▶ Players try to be the team with the highest number of
points at the end of the game. The maximum score for
each player, if all skittles were knocked down in one
turn, would be:

$$55 = 10+9+8+7+6+5+4+3+2+1$$

Variations Players in the teams can also challenge
each other to knock down particular skittles. A point is
won for every correct skittle knocked down. The
maximum score would be 10 points.

JUMP THE ROPE

Number The game is best played with a large number of players (at least five) who are all fairly nimble.

Place and time It can be played outdoors at any time or indoors in a large hall.

Equipment A rope about 4 metres long is needed. It should have a soft weight, such as a pencil rubber, tied on to it at one end.

How to play ▶ Players form a wide circle. One player stands in the middle. She swings the rope round and round (**A**) at about the height of the players' ankles. ▶ The players have to jump over the rope as it comes round their way (**B**). Anyone who fails to jump over the rope is out and takes a turn at swinging the rope.

SKITTLE THEM OUT

Number Ten players, of any age, play in two teams of five.

Place and time The game is played outdoors on a flat surface at any time, preferably in fine weather.

Equipment Five plastic bottles, half-full of water and closed tight, are used as skittles. Two plastic footballs, and chalk or rope to mark a circle, are also needed.

Preparation A circle about 4 metres in diameter is marked out.

How to play ▶ One team stands inside the circle, with each member beside a skittle standing on the ground. ▶ The opposing team must stay outside the circle and throw the plastic balls at the skittles, aiming to knock them down (**A**). As the balls are thrown, they are picked up by another player on the throwing team. ▶ The defending team members try to intercept the balls and protect their skittles. They may not touch any skittle, nor stand over it. ▶ When a skittle is knocked down, the player and his skittle leave the circle. ▶ Players aim to get all the defending team out of the circle. When this is achieved, teams change places.

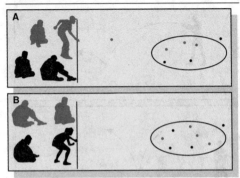

MARBLES

Number The game is for two or more players, forming teams.

Place and time It is played indoors or outdoors on a flat surface in dry weather.

Equipment Five or six marbles per player and chalk are needed.

Preparation A circle, 1 metre in diameter, is drawn for each team. A start line is drawn about 4 metres from each circle.

How to play ▶ Team members, in turn, roll their marbles from the start line into the circle (**A**). If a marble misses or knocks another marble out, the marble outside the circle is retrieved by the player who owns it.

▶ Players try to be the first to get all their marbles in the circle (**B**).

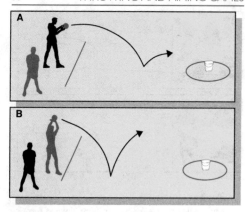

BUCKET BALL

Number Two or more players of any age can play in two equal teams.

Place and time The game is played outdoors in dry weather.

Equipment A large bucket and a plastic football-sized ball, a scoreboard (or a non-playing score-keeper), some chalk and a timer are needed.

Preparation The bucket should be set in a fixed position on the ground. A chalk line is marked around the bucket within which nobody may step. A line should be marked on the ground about 20 metres from the bucket. This is the starting line.

How to play ▶ A member of the first team stands on

the starting point and tries to throw the ball so that it bounces once and then enters the bucket (**A**). If the ball lands in the bucket, that team gets 1 point and the opposite team takes the ball to the starting line for a throw (**B**). ▶ If the ball does not land in the bucket, the first player (from either team) to get the ball (**C**), without stepping into the circle, takes a throw from the starting line (**D**). ▶ The ball may be thrown from player to player to get it back to the starting line without the other team stealing it. It may not be kicked. Players must stand still while they are holding the ball. ▶ The game continues for an agreed time limit. ▶ The team with the highest score at the end of the game wins.

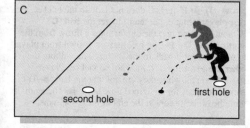

PEBBLE GOLF

Number This game is for two or more players of any age.

Place and time It can be played on a sandy beach in fine weather.

Equipment Each player needs one small pebble about 2–3 centimetres in diameter.

Preparation A starting line is drawn on the ground and a small hole, about the size of one of the pebbles, is dug about 10 metres away from it.

How to play ▶ Each player in turn stands on the starting line and attempts to throw her pebble into the hole (**A**). Each player throws only once in her turn. If she misses the hole she has to wait until the next round to try again from the spot where the pebble landed.
▶ To make a throw, a player must hold the pebble cupped in both hands with fingers clasped together and toss the pebble without breaking the clasp. ▶ Any player whose pebble lands in the hole wins a point (**B**). If two or more players get their pebbles in, they each win a point. ▶ This first hole is then used as the starting line for the second hole, which is dug about 10 metres away from the first hole. ▶ The game proceeds as before (**C**), until a total of nine holes are played. The winner is the player with the highest number of points. In the case of a draw, there is a play-off to decide the final winner.

3. Racing games

BUMP ON THE BACK

Number This is a good game for two or three families to play together, and will be most enjoyable with ten or more people.

Place and time Play this game outdoors in dry weather on a camp site, in a field or on the beach.

Equipment None.

How to play ▶ One person is chosen to start the game. The rest form a circle (**A**) and then sit on the ground. ▶ The chosen person moves clockwise round the outside of the circle, behind the players. He touches one of them gently on the back and then continues

running round the circle. ▶ The player who has been touched must now get up and run in the opposite direction, i.e. counterclockwise (**B**). They both aim to get back to the space left by the touched player. Whoever gets there first sits in the place and the other goes around the outside again.

Variation This game can also be played by using a handkerchief to drop behind the selected player. The aim is to gain advantage by dropping the handkerchief almost unseen, so that the runner completes the circuit unopposed until he reaches the handkerchief.

LETTERS

Number This game needs three or more players.

Place and time It can be played indoors in a hall or outdoors at any time.

Equipment Chalk, rope or piles of coats can be used to mark the play area.

Preparation The play area is marked out on the ground by two parallel lines 3 metres apart. One person, the caller, stands behind one line.
The others all line up opposite the caller behind the other parallel line.

How to play ▶ The caller calls out one letter of the alphabet. ▶ Any player who has that letter anywhere in his first name, middle name or surname takes one step (or jump) forward (**A**). The caller continues calling out letters and the players take steps forward (**B**). ▶ If the letter occurs twice in a name, two steps forward are allowed (**C**). ▶ Generally, the caller tries to avoid repeating letters. ▶ The player who reaches the other parallel line first and can touch the caller (**D**) is the winner and becomes the next caller. ▶ Although this is

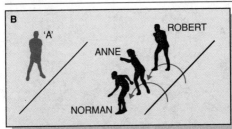

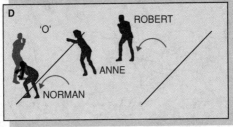

a very slow race, the fun lies in the information revealed, such as discovering that someone has a second name with a Q in it.

Variations The caller can use different categories to call out – for example:

RELATIONS – here, names are called out and anyone having a relative with that name can take a step forward;

COLOURS – different colours are called and anyone wearing that colour, or having it on his body, can move forward;

WHAT DID YOU HAVE FOR BREAKFAST? – the caller asks, 'Did you have?'. . . and calls different foods;

MAY I ? – this is another variation in which the caller tells each player in turn to take particular kinds of steps. The player must say 'May I?' before proceeding or she has to go back to the start.

Special names can be given to the different kinds of steps, and the caller can make up names. For example:

Banana slip (**A**) – sliding one foot as far forward as possible and drawing the other up to it.

Frog jump (**B**) – jumping from a crouching position.

Bucket (**C**) – stepping through one's own joined hands.

Pin (**D**) – stepping on the points of the toes.

Caterpillar (**E**) – moving forward by lying on the

E

ground and moving forward without lifting the head.
Fairy step (**F**) – making a small, heel-to-toe step.
Bunny rabbit (**G**) – hopping with both feet together.
Scissors – jumping with feet apart and again bringing
feet together.
Lamppost – lying down forwards on the ground and
standing again where fingers reached.
Trip round the moon – taking player, with eyes shut,
wherever caller likes by calling out directions.
Lotus walk (**H**) – walking on knees until told to stop.
Soldier – stepping with body held stiff.

Umbrella – twisting round while taking a step forward.
Giant stride (**I**) – taking as long a step as possible.
To London and back – running to and fro between the
player in front and the start line until told to stop.
Policeman's walk – (both player and caller) closing eyes
as player walks forward until caller shouts 'Stop!'
Cabbage (**J**) – taking a step in a crouching position with
arms clutched around body.
Old man – taking a step forward in a bent position as if
using a walking stick.

PUSS IN THE CORNER

Number The game is for five players, but more can play.

Place and time It is played indoors or outdoors at any time of the year.

Equipment None.

Preparations Four of the players take up four positions in the playing area, which then become the four 'safe places'; these are, for example, the four corners of a room or four circles marked out in the sand on a beach (**A**). The fifth player is the catcher and can move anywhere in the area of play.

How to play ▶ The four players have to keep running from one safe place to another (**B**). ▶ The

catcher has to try to get onto an empty safe place. ▶ When the catcher does this, the player without a safe place becomes the next catcher. ▶ The skill in this game is to dart to and fro and make quick changes of direction to confuse others into leaving an empty safe place. ▶ If the catcher thinks a player has been standing on a safe place too long without moving, the catcher can then call 'All change.' Then, all four players must move to another safe place immediately.

Variation

If there are more than five players, more safe places will be needed. However, if there are ten or more players, two games can run simultaneously.

HOT PEAS

Number Any number from four upwards can play this game.

Place and time It is played wherever there is plenty of space outdoors, and in dry weather.

Equipment None.

Preparation A home base is chosen, such as a lamppost, a particular rock or a mound in a field. One person is chosen as caller. This person closes his eyes and faces the home base. The other players stand behind him (**A**), hands on top of each other's and placed on the caller's back.

How to play ▶ The caller names a person and tells

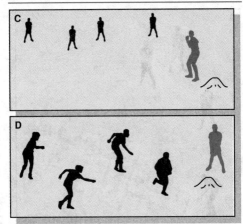

her to go to a particular place, such as the gate, the paddling pool, the pond, the tree, etc. ▶ The player then removes her hand from the caller's back and goes to her position (**B**). ▶ The caller continues, naming everyone in any order and giving each one a place to go to. ▶ When everyone is in place, the caller opens his eyes and turns round (**C**). He begins shouting, 'Hot potatoes . . . hot gravy . . . hot chicken . . . hot prunes . . . hot pickles . . .' and so on. ▶ Nobody moves until he shouts 'Hot peas', then all players run as fast as they can back to the home base (**D**). The last one home is slapped on the back and becomes the next caller.

HOPSCOTCH

Number This game is for any number of players. One person can even play against herself. Players can play against each other or in two teams.

Place and time It is played outdoors on a pavement or other surface that can be marked. It is best played in dry weather.

Equipment A small, flat stone is needed, as well as a piece of chalk for marking the ground.

Preparation A hopscotch area is marked out on the

ground as in the diagram (**A**). The squares are then numbered, and a starting line is drawn about one hop from the first square.

How to play ▶ The first player slides the flat stone onto the square marked 1 (**B**). ▶ He then jumps over square 1 to land with his left foot in square 2 and his right foot in square 3 (**C**). ▶ He hops onto square 4, and then jumps and hops his way to squares 11 and 12, where he turns by jumping to land with a foot in each square. He then hops and jumps back to the start.

When he reaches squares 2 and 3, he must pick up the stone from square 1 and leap over it. ▶ If he does this correctly, he then throws the stone onto square 2, hops onto squares 1, 3 and 4 (**D**), and then proceeds as before. ▶ On his way back, he picks up the stone, while balancing on one leg on square 3. ▶ The player continues until making a mistake, such as:
– not sliding the stone fully onto the square (**E**)
– putting a foot onto the wrong square

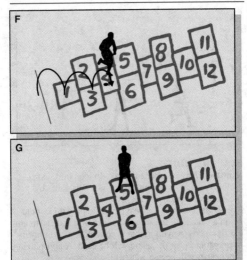

– landing on the square with the stone in it (**F**)
– losing his balance and putting a foot down when he should be on one leg only (**G**)
– the player fails to jump (or hop) to turn round for the return journey. ▶ If a player fails to reach the end, he has to wait until other players have had a go. He then re-enters the game at the point where he failed before.

▶ The players take turns until one wins by reaching number 12 and returning without making any mistakes.

HOP AND BUILD

Number Any number can play, divided into teams. However, even two people can enjoy this game by racing against each other.

Place and time The best places to play this would be on a beach, on the shore of a lake or beside a stream.

Equipment Anything that is collected by the players in preparation for the game will be used. A non-playing timekeeper will need a watch.

Preparation Each team selects a spot, near the other team, as the site for its team dump (marked X in diagram **A**). At the word 'Go', the timekeeper gives the players five minutes to scavenge the beach or shoreline for any loose materials that can be used for building, such as sand, soil, rocks, pebbles, shells, twigs and general flotsam – for instance, bits of wood or drinks cans. Teams stand ready at their dump site. Players must use only their hands – rather than, say, a bag – to carry their materials back to their team dump (**A**).

There is no limit to how much building material is collected.

When the timekeeper has called time-up, each team claims a building site, 10 metres away from their dump. The building sites, which are marked with a twig or stone, do not have to be close to each other.

How to play ▶ Each team lines up near its dump of building materials. ▶ The timekeeper decides how much time will be available for teams to build any kind of construction (which has been decided on beforehand), realistic or imaginative, using only the collected materials. Ten minutes should be adequate.

▶ On the word 'Go', the first players in each team take any items they can carry from their dump to their building sites (**B**). They must hop all the way, and any materials dropped en route are to be considered lost.

▶ When the player reaches the building site, she starts the construction (**C**), as shown overleaf, then hops back to her team (**D**). The next player on the team may only

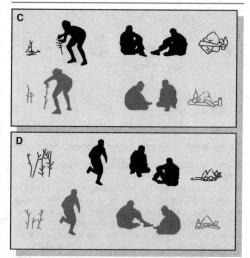

pick up building materials when he has been touched by the first player on her return. ▶ The second player then hops to the building site, carrying the chosen materials, adds them to the construction (**E**) and hops back to touch the third player. ▶ Players can make a second trip to the site, to carry materials or make adjustments to the construction. This continues until the time is up (**F**). ▶ The timekeeper decides the winning team by choosing which he thinks is the best construction.

Variations *1* The timekeeper can state in advance
what kind of construction is to be made.
2 If a watch is not available to time the contest, the
winning team will be the one to use up all its materials
first.
3 If the game is played on a camp site, the materials for
building could include some of the equipment usually
taken on a camping holiday, such as plastic bottles, cups
and picnic baskets or lunch boxes.

LINE ROUNDERS

Number Six or more players in two teams can play.

Place and time It is played any time outdoors, and preferably in a large space, such as a field.

Equipment A soft ball is needed.

Preparation The members of one team line up behind each other (**A**), standing close together. They are the batters. The other team scatters around the playing area as fielders, except for one of the members who is

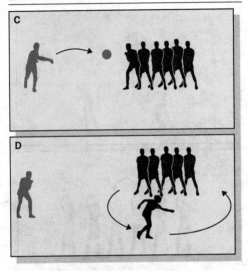

the bowler (**B**). The bowler stands facing the batting team, which is about 2 metres away.

How to play ▶ The bowler throws the ball to the first batter who hits it with her closed fist as far as she can (**C**). The first batter then runs around her team (**D**), even if she hasn't hit the ball. She keeps on running round the team until she hears a fielder shout 'Stop!' ▶ The fielders, meanwhile, try to retrieve the ball as quickly as possible. Whoever touches it first has to stand still

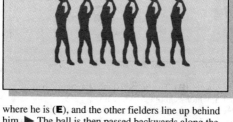

where he is (**E**), and the other fielders line up behind him. ▶ The ball is then passed backwards along the line of fielders, who throw it overhead. When the last fielder in line gets it, she shouts 'Stop!'(**F**). ▶ The batter must then stop running and join the end of her team, leaving the next person ready to bat. The bowling and batting continue as before. Any of the fielders can

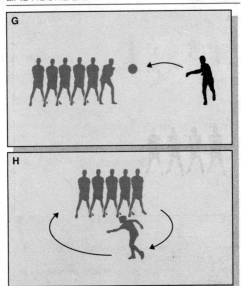

act as bowler. ▶ When all the batting team have had a turn at running, the teams change places (**G** and **H**).
Scoring Each batter scores 1 point for each complete run made round the team. Players try to be the team with the greatest number of runs after both teams have batted. To continue the game, players might agree on additional batting rounds for each team.

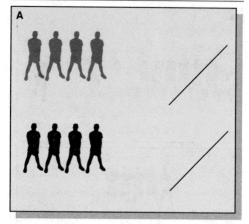

HEAD RACE
Number This game is for any number of players of any age in two equal teams.

Place and time It is played indoors or outdoors in dry weather.

Equipment Each participant needs a similar object that can be carried on the head. They might be, for example, towels (each tied into a tight knot), empty drinks cans, books or folded newspapers, beach bags or small, flat pebbles.

A finishing line can be marked with rope or coats.

How to play ▶ Teams line up at one end of a race course measuring about 10 – 20 metres long. At the far

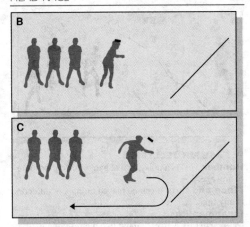

end is the finishing line (**A**). ▶ The first player in each team walks to the finishing line, balancing the object on his head (**B**). ▶ If an object is dropped, the player has to return to the start (**C**). ▶ Once a member of a team has reached the line, the next person in that team can proceed. The winning team is the one that completes the course first.

Variation Placing obstacles in the way can make the course more interesting. Indoors, this could be furniture that has to be climbed over or under. Outdoors, it could be objects, such as walls, gates and hills, which have to be navigated.

PLEASE MR JELLYFISH

Number This is a noisy, active game for four or more of any age.

Place and time It can be played indoors or outdoors at any time.

Equipment None.

Preparation A 'river' about two metres wide is marked across the playing area. This can be done by scratching in soft ground or by agreeing which paving stones or tiles mark the banks of the river. If indoors, players can use piles of coats or other objects to mark the banks.

One person is chosen to be Mr Jellyfish.

All the other players stand on one side of the river, while Mr Jellyfish stands on the opposite side, facing them (**A**).

How to play ▶ Players call out together, 'Please Mr Jellyfish, may we cross your river?'

Mr Jellyfish replies, 'You may cross if . . .' and states the condition, for example:

– if you are wearing green;
– if you had egg for breakfast;
– if you have some string in your pocket; and so on.
► Mr Jellyfish can challenge players to prove they
fulfil the condition. ► Anyone who satisfies Mr
Jellyfish is allowed to walk across. Those who are left
repeat the game. ► After the third condition has been
given, any player who has not yet crossed the river must
then make a run for it. If the player is caught (**B**), she
becomes the new Mr Jellyfish. ► If nobody is caught,
the same person continues to be Mr Jellyfish. For
players to get back to their starting side of the river, they
must do so without being caught by Mr Jellyfish. ► If
they all get back safely, this Mr Jellyfish must retire and
a new Mr Jellyfish is chosen. The next choice could be
the one whose birthday comes next.

A 'GRUNT' 'PIG' 'GRUNT'

ZOO

Number This noisy, active game is for eight or more players in two equal teams, plus one person playing the leader.

Place and time It is played outdoors at any time.

Equipment Only a watch is needed.

Preparation Players set up a race course about 20 metres long with starting and finishing lines marked in the ground or using stones or coats. A length of time for the game is then agreed on, and the person with the watch is asked to call 'Time's up' when the end of the game is reached.

How to play ▶ The teams line up and each member is given the name of an animal. The first players in each team are given the same animal name, as are the second

players, and so on. ▶ The leader stands at the finishing line and calls the name of one of the animals. ▶ The player from each team who is that animal has to run to the finishing line and back, making the noise of their animals (**A**). ▶ The leader calls again, and another pair race against each other, making the appropriate noises. If the leader shouts 'Zoo', everyone has to run (**B**) making animal noises.

Scoring The first player of each pair to get back to the starting line gets 1 point. The first team to get back when 'Zoo' has been shouted scores 10 points. Teams aim to win the most points after a given time.

Variations Other subjects can be used – for example:
– musical instruments (singing or dancing); or
– transport (making car, train or plane sounds).

ODDS AND EVENS

Number Three or more people can play this game.
Place and time It is suitable for outdoors in a field
or on a beach, and can be played at any time.
Equipment None.
Preparation Two parallel lines about 3 metres apart
are marked out on the ground or sand; this area is called
'the street'. A caller is chosen and stands on one side of
the street. All the other players stand on the other side
(**A**).
How to play ▶ The caller calls out any number,
either odd or even – for example:
7 odd; 22 odd; 4 even; 63 odd, and so on. ▶ When
'odd' is called with an odd number, or 'even' with an
even number, everyone has to run across the street and

back to the original positions (**B**). ▶ If 'even' is called with an odd number or 'odd' with an even number, nobody should run. ▶ Anyone who runs when she should not is out (**C**). When a player is out, that person becomes the new caller. When another person is out and becomes caller, the previous caller sits away from the playing area (**D**). ▶ It is good strategy to make calls quickly one after another so that players get confused and make wrong moves. ▶ The aim is to stay in the game as long as possible.

Variation If a watch is available, a caller can be challenged to get everyone out within a given time limit. If this variation is played, the caller is not replaced during the game.

A

PASS THE ORANGE
Number The game is for eight or more players in two equal teams.
Place and time It is played outdoors in fine weather, or indoors.
Equipment Two oranges or objects of similar size, such as tennis balls, are needed.
How to play ▶ Each team stands close together in a line. The team leader puts an orange under his chin (**A**), holding it in place between his chin and chest. On a call of 'Go' from a non-player, the leader then has to pass the orange to the next player in his team without dropping it. Nobody can touch the orange with either

hands or feet. ▶ If a player drops the orange (**B**), it has to go back to the leader, who begins again (**C**). ▶ The third time the orange is dropped, it can go to the other end of the line to give the other players a chance to play. ▶ The first team to pass its orange along all its members without dropping it is the winner.

Variations Players can race to pass things in other ways. Players can, for example, sit down in a line or a circle and pass a pebble by cradling it between their feet so that each person has to swing her legs above the next player's legs and gently drop the pebble onto the other's feet.

4. Collecting games

COLOUR SCHEMES

Number Two or more can play this game.

Place and Time It can be played indoors anywhere or outdoors in a garden in fine weather.

Equipment You will need a selection of coloured pictures cut from old magazines or postcards; a pencil and paper for each person; and a watch for timing the game.

How to play ▶ The pictures are collected together in a pile and shuffled (**A**). ▶ Each person then takes a picture from the bottom of the pile and makes a list on paper of the colours in his picture. ▶ Players then go off to find objects which are as near as possible the

C	COLOUR	OBJECT
	YELLOW	TENT
	GREEN	LEAVES
	RED	BUCKET
	BLACK	FENCE
	PINK	
	BLUE	

same colours as those in the picture (**B**). ▶ When an object is found that matches a colour, the player finding it writes the name of the object opposite the colour on his paper (**C**). ▶ A time limit of, say, ten minutes is given. ▶ The aim is to complete a list of objects in the given time. Each person has to explain to the others which colours corresponded to which objects.

Variation Players can be required to find an object for each colour and to bring it back, instead of merely writing down its name. This could mean finding leaves, pebbles and other items; but, of course, nothing should be stolen or picked!

A

The new one for Spring — by popular demand!

GROWING PAINS?
WE HAVE THE REMEDY!

Hats off to Shirley!

A day at the Bookfair

From strength to strength for the lion

HEADLINES

Number This game is for one or more playing individually. It is suitable for people who enjoy playing with words.

Place and time It is played anywhere indoors. It can also be played outdoors in warm weather in a sheltered spot.

Equipment You will need one or more newspapers, a watch, and a pencil and paper for each player.

How to play ▶ Each player selects five headlines at random from a newspaper (**A**). ▶ Each player then writes down as many new headlines as possible using the words from his original headlines. The words can be reorganized in any arrangement; they do not need to

B

A DAY FOR HATS OFF
THE STRENGTH OF POPULAR DEMAND
A REMEDY FOR PAINS
POPULAR SHIRLEY FOR ONE DAY
THE LION AT THE BOOK FAIR
DEMAND FOR SPRING GROWING
NEW STRENGTH FOR HATS
SPRING OFF FROM STRENGTH

be complete sentences (**B**). ▶ After five minutes,
players compare their new headlines, and the one with
the most wins.

Variation If a newspaper is not available, players
could go for a walk and collect ten words from
advertisements seen in shops or on billboards.
Collecting the words or phrases from billboards is an
extra challenge if the player is in a foreign country.

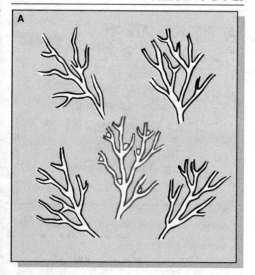

ODD ONE OUT

Number This game is for four or more people. Two can play, but the game is more interesting with more players.

Place and time It can be played indoors or outdoors in dry weather.

Equipment None.

How to play ▶ Each person goes off to find a set of five objects, four of which should be exactly the same.

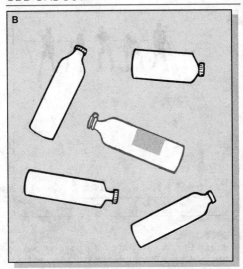

The fifth should be the odd one out – for example, five twigs, only one of which has buds (**A**) (but live twigs should not be picked); five bottles (**B**), only one of which is glass; or five corks, only one of which is for a wine bottle, etc. ▶ On their return, all the players display their objects. The others have to say which is the odd one out in each player's set of five. ▶ The aim is to find a set of five in which the difference of the odd one is so subtle that everyone has difficulty in identifying it.

FREE FOR ALL

Number Three or more players of any age can play.

Place and time It is suitable for indoors or outdoors in fine weather. A playing area should be agreed on and marked out.

Equipment A plastic shopping bag, a beach bag or some other kind of bag or basket is needed. Otherwise, a towel held by the corners would be adequate.

You also need 12 objects of assorted sizes (**A**). These can be balls, balls of wool, screwed up pieces of newspaper, empty drinks cans and anything that players might have in their pockets, such as a comb, a pencil or a bunch of keys.

How to play ▶ One person is chosen to carry the bag of objects and has to move around the playing area. ▶ As she moves, she attempts to get rid of all the objects from the bag by picking them out by hand, one by one, and dropping them (**B**). She may not tip the bag or shake it to bounce the objects out. ▶ The other players have to stop her from emptying the bag by picking up the objects and putting them back in the bag (**C**). ▶ The aim of the game is for the player with the bag to empty it. When the player achieves this, she can choose the next person to have the bag. All the objects should, of course, be collected up at the end of the game.

BEAN-HIDING

Number This is for four or more players of any age.

Place and time It can be played at home, on a camp site or beach, or in the country – and at any time in dry weather.

Equipment You will need a supply of small objects, such as dried beans, acorns, conkers or shells (**A**). Alternatively, you could use marbles if they are available. A watch will also be needed.

How to play ▶ One person is chosen as the hider. The other players, the seekers, stay near a home base while the hider goes off to hide the objects (**B**). ▶ He hides them in different places within an agreed area. In each place, he may vary the number of beans he deposits between one and three. ▶ The hider returns to

the home base (**C**). ▶ He then tells the seekers that they
have a set amount of time (which can be varied
according to the size of the play area) to find the beans.
They run off to try to find as many beans as possible
(**D**). They may take *all* the beans from any hiding place
they find. The hider times the seekers. The winner is the
player with the highest number of beans at the end of
the appointed time.

PICTURE QUIZ

Number In this game, two or more players compete against each other. It is a quiet game requiring concentration, and is suitable for children who love a quiz, and can read and write.

Place and time It is played indoors in wet weather or outside in fine weather. Players will need a flat surface, such as a picnic table, on which to play.

Equipment Each player needs a pencil, a picture on a piece of card – such as that cut or torn from an empty cereal packet – and a sheet of paper the same size. Both the card and the sheet of paper should be about A4 size. Alternatively, if scissors and glue are available, a magazine picture can be stuck onto a piece of cardboard. If only pencil and paper are available, each player will need two sheets of paper, and could draw her own picture on one of the sheets.

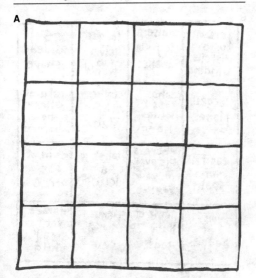

Preparation Each player divides the back of her picture into 16 sections by drawing three equally spaced lines down and across the back. The sheet of paper is also divided into 16 sections in exactly the same way (**A**). Players should make these preparations where their papers cannot be seen by the others.

Each player then thinks up 16 questions with short answers. One question is written in each of the 16

B

person who installs windows	noise a dog makes	longest river in world	5 sided shape
largest planet	who was King Kong	type of deer	ratio of miles to kilometres
capital of Spain	where is the pupil in your body	what is a KIWI	skin of a tree
type of pudding	name of baby goat	name for a ball	name for small child

spaces marked on the plain paper (**B**).

The answers are written on the back of the picture in the *opposite* 16 spaces (**C**), *not* the corresponding ones, so that the answer sheet is a mirror-image of the question sheet.

The picture is then cut or torn into 16 pieces along the marked lines, and the pieces are kept together neatly in a pile. The paper with the questions is left whole.

How to play ▶ Players come together when their

c

PENTAGON	NILE	growl	glazier
1·5	moose	a movie gorilla	JUPITER
BARK	a Bird	in your eye	MADRID
Toddler	sphere	kid	mousse

questions and answers are ready. ▶ They exchange their sheets of questions and the cut-up answers. ▶ Each player has to fit the correct answers, with the writing facing upwards, onto the question sheet in the correct places. ▶ The players then turn the answers over individually. If the answers are placed in the right positions, the picture will be correctly reassembled!

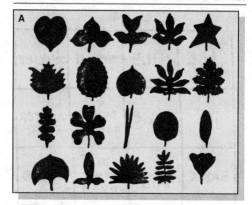

NATURE SCAVENGE

Number The game is for two or more players. If there is a large number, two or more teams can be formed.

Place and time It is played outdoors in fine weather, and is especially good for a park or beach.

Equipment Each player or team needs paper and a pencil, as well as a bucket or plastic bag. A watch for timing the game will be needed.

Preparation Each player, or team, writes down a list of 12 things that another player or team has to find. The lists should be of natural things that will not be damaged by collection, such as a variety of different shapes of fallen leaves (**A, B**) or dead marine creatures or plants (**C, D** over page).

The lists can be general, such as one asking for 12

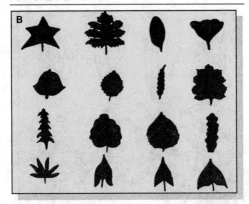

leaves of different shapes, or it can be more specific, such as one listing the types of shell to be collected (**D** over page). Lists should not include anything that must be picked from a live plant, and any live creatures, such as tiny crabs or shellfish, should be returned to the place where you found them once the game is over.

How to play ▶ When the lists are ready, they are exchanged and players or teams set off to find the items on their list. ▶ Players are given a time limit of, for example, three minutes. They can time themselves with their own watches, or one player can act as timekeeper for all players. ▶ When the time limit is up, everyone returns to where they started. The teams or players display their collections, which are checked against the lists and either accepted or rejected by the list-maker(s).

13 different types of seaweed

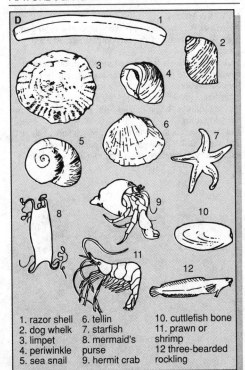

1. razor shell
2. dog whelk
3. limpet
4. periwinkle
5. sea snail
6. tellin
7. starfish
8. mermaid's purse
9. hermit crab
10. cuttlefish bone
11. prawn or shrimp
12 three-bearded rockling

LETTER HUNT

Number Any number of players aged 9 or older can play. A minimum of two can compete against each other.

Place and time It is played indoors or outdoors at any time of the year. Any interesting site can be used for observation – for example, a university college (**A**), a garden, a museum, a castle (**B**), a farmyard, etc. If playing indoors, be polite and follow the rules about not touching things.

Equipment Each player needs a watch and a pencil and paper. It is a good game for expanding your vocabulary, especially when played using a guide book

A

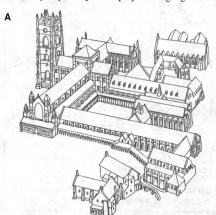

or some other source of new names for objects.

How to play ▶ A non-player should act as time-keeper. ▶ The time-keeper chooses any category – for example, furniture, the colour blue, or items made of wood – and starts the game by announcing the category. ▶ Players are allowed a set time, perhaps 15 minutes, to explore the site, aiming to find and write down the names of as many things in that category as they can see. ▶ Players aim to find an appropriate object beginning with each letter of the alphabet. ▶ At the end of the time limit, players return to the starting point and compare their lists. The player whose list includes the most objects starting with a different letter wins.

B

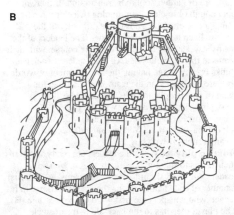

MEMORY CHASE

Number This is a game for eight or more players in two teams competing against each other.

Place and time It is an outdoor game to be played where there are plenty of obstacles to climb or jump over, such as on a rocky beach, in a field with little mounds, or in a picnic area with seats and tables.

Equipment None.

Preparation The players must first agree on an obstacle course, about 10–12 metres long. The length should be adjusted to suit local conditions. The obstacles are agreed on – perhaps rocks to be jumped over, a wall to be climbed or a piece of outdoor furniture or garden pool to be run around. If there are not enough obstacles, then running twice or three times round a tree or a rock adds to the difficulty of the course. Each team chooses a leader. The leaders of the teams stand at one end of the obstacle course, with their teams at the opposite side (**A**). The leader of each team thinks up a message having the same number of words as there are players in the team. For example, for a team of five people, the message could be:
– six pink elephants running wild . . . or
– large purple cloud descending rapidly . . . or
– local mayor visiting Wonderland today . . . or
– camel runs off with boy.

How to play ▶ When the leaders are ready, they tell their teams to stand in line, ready to run. ▶ The leaders, together, shout 'Go' to their teams. ▶ The first member of each team runs via the obstacle course to his leader, who whispers the first word of the message (**B**). The player then has to run back along the obstacle

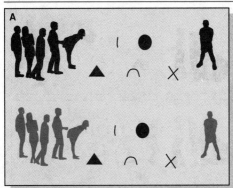

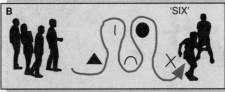

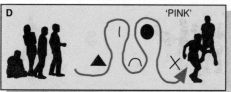

D   'PINK'

E   'SIX PINK'

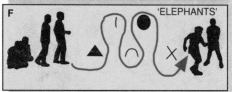

F   'ELEPHANTS'

G   'SIX PINK ELEPHANTS'

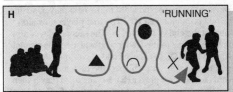

'SIX PINK ELEPHANTS RUNNING'

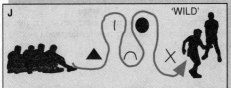

course and whisper the word to the next player, so that
the others cannot hear (**C**). The first player now sits
down at the end of the line. ▶ The second player now
runs the course to the leader who whispers the second
word to him (**D**). ▶ The second player runs the course,
back to his team, and whispers the first and second
words to the third player (**E**). ▶ The third player then
runs the course to collect the third word (**F, G**) . . . and
so on (**H, I, J**). ▶ The game proceeds in this way until
all members have run and collected words. The last
player must get back to his team before he shouts out
the whole message (**K**). ▶ If the message is correct, the
leader shouts 'Well done.' If not, the leader says which
word is wrong – for example, 'Second word wrong.' In
this case, the second player has to run again to collect
the second word and pass it to the last member, who
then shouts out the corrected message.

The first team to shout out the correct message is the
winner. Teams then choose a new leader, who thinks up
a new message.

SCOTS AND ENGLISH

Number The game is for eight or more players, divided into two equal teams.

Place and time It is played outdoors in dry weather.

Equipment A selection of non-fragile personal property is required, such as coats, hats, bats, balls, shoes, books, comics, sweets, etc.

Preparation Teams gather on opposite sides of a natural divide, such as a narrow, shallow stream, a trench dug in the sand, a low fence or low wall.

Each member of the team puts two or three personal articles into the team's pool of property. The team then stands facing the opposition with their property spread out before them (**A**).

Behind each pile of articles, a small area is marked out to represent the home base.

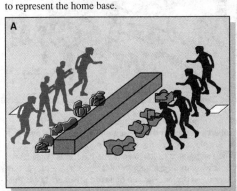

How to play ▶ Players must try to capture all the property of the opposing team and protect their own (**B**). ▶ A player may only take one item at a time. ▶ When she gets it to her own home base, it is considered safe and cannot be recaptured (**C**). ▶ Once a player has crossed the divide, she can be taken prisoner (**D**). If this happens, she is made to stand near the capturing team's

home base (**E**) and must be rescued – that is, brought
back to her own home base by her team members –
before any more property can be taken.

Each team tries to get all the opposing team's property
to its own home base, or to capture all members of the
opposing team.

5. Guessing and remembering games

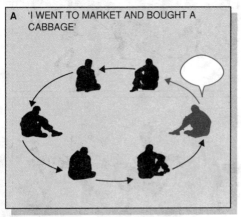

A 'I WENT TO MARKET AND BOUGHT A CABBAGE'

I WENT TO MARKET
Number Two or more people of any age can play.
Place and time The game is played indoors, or outdoors in fine weather.
How to play ▶ Everyone sits in a circle and the first person says, 'I went to market and bought . . . ', for example, 'a cabbage' (**A**). ▶ The next person, on her right, has to repeat 'cabbage' and add an item of his own, such as 'a lamp' (**B**). ▶ Each player continues to

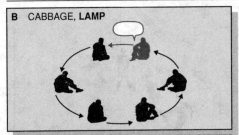

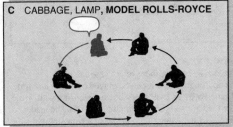

add a new item, and repeats the list so far, until someone forgets an item, and has to drop out. The last one in is the winner and starts the next round. ▶ The list can be odd and difficult, for example: 'I went to market and bought a cabbage; a lamp; a model Rolls-Royce (**C**); six pounds of new potatoes; a red and blue parrot in a cage; four very large cucumbers; a bunch of flowers containing roses, geraniums, daisies and lilies; a green box of China tea', and so on . . . .

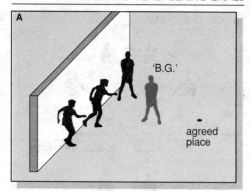

POP STARS

Number Four or more of any age can play.

Place and time It can be played outdoors any time.

How to play ▶ Players line up against a wall while the leader stands about a metre away. ▶ The leader thinks of the name of a pop star or a film star and calls out the initials (**A**). ▶ Anyone who thinks she has guessed who it is runs to an agreed place and back to the leader (**B**) and tells him who she thinks it is. ▶ If she is correct, they change places. If not, the player returns to the line. ▶ Players keep trying to guess the answers; if they give up, the leader is able to keep his position.

Variations Instead of using pop stars, the leader can use the initials of newspapers. He may say, 'I sent my son John to the newsagent to buy a copy of (for

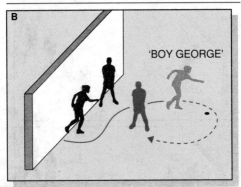

example) the N.O.T.W. (News Of The World).' A player who thinks she has guessed what it is, runs as before, and tells the leader. If correct, she becomes the new leader.

Leaders could also choose items and give a clue to them by saying where they are to be found – for example, 'I sent my son John to:

– the chemist to buy a B.O.C.M. (Bottle of Cough Mixture)';

– the corner shop to get a P.O.D.B. (Packet Of Dog Biscuits)';

– the pet shop to buy T.B.M. (Three Blind Mice).'

The game can also be played in front of a shop window, when the leader might say, 'I can see a G.J.W.R.S. (Green Jumper With Red Stripes).'

STROKE THE BABY

Number The game is for at least four players, usually younger children.

Place and time It can be played anywhere, and at any time.

Preparation You will need a scarf or large, clean handkerchief as a blindfold.

How to play ▶ One player is blindfolded and made to face a wall (**A**). ▶ The other players creep up behind him, one player strokes his back, and they then creep back (**B**). ▶ After counting out loud to 10, the

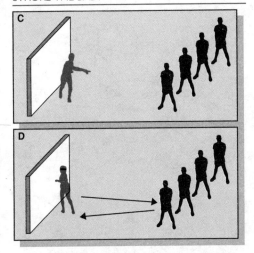

blindfolded player removes his blindfold, turns round and points at the person he thinks touched him (**C**). If he is correct, that person takes his place and turns to face the wall (**D**).

Variations Sometimes the blindfolded player has to say which hand or even which finger was used to stroke him.

The person facing the wall does not need to be blindfolded; he may just be required to close his eyes.

A

MONEY BAG

Number The game is for two, or more, teams of at least two players each. People of any age can enjoy this game.

Place and time It can be played indoors or out.

Equipment Each team needs a piece of lightweight fabric or a paper bag about 20 cm square and a selection of five or six small coins and a few buttons or tokens. The bags must not be transparent. A tie or piece of string will be needed to close them. Pencil and paper are also needed to keep a record.

B

Preparation Each team, in private, first writes down a list of their coins and other objects, puts them into the bag or piece of fabric, and then ties the top.

How to play ▶ Teams pass their bags, in turn, to the other teams (**A**), who have to feel the objects inside (**B**), identify them and state the value of each coin. ▶ When all teams have had a turn with each bag, the bags are opened and the contents checked. ▶ The aim of the game is for players to guess all the contents correctly. The team with the most correct guesses wins.

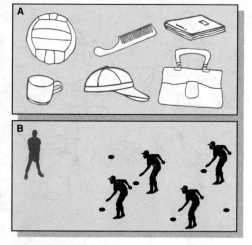

BLINDFOLD SEARCH

Number The game is for three or more players of any age competing against each other.

Place and time It is played indoors, or outdoors in dry weather where there is a clear, flat area.

Equipment Five or six articles such as a ball, hat, bag, comb, book or cup are needed (**A**), as well as a timer and a blindfold.

Preparation Players decide the order of play. One player must act as timekeeper. The first player watches as the others place the articles on the ground (**B**).

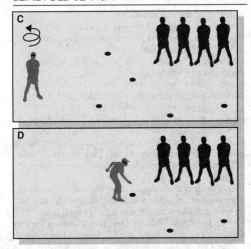

The first player is then blindfolded and turned round
twice on the spot (**C**).

How to play ▶ One player shouts 'Begin' and starts
to time the game. ▶ The blindfolded player is allowed ten
seconds to locate and pick up all the articles (**D**) before
the timekeeper calls 'Stop'. ▶ The player scores points
for the number of articles picked up. ▶ Then it is the
turn of the next player, and so on. ▶ Players may agree
to have one turn each or several turns each before the
game ends. ▶ The player with the most points is the
winner.

BLINDFOLD DRAWING

Number Four or more players of any age can play.

Place and time It is played indoors at any time, or outdoors in fine weather.

Equipment Each player needs a pencil, piece of paper and a blindfold.

Preparation One player is chosen to be the caller. All other players put on their blindfolds and hold their pencils and paper at the ready (**A**).

How to play ▶ The caller instructs the players to draw something, bit by bit – for example, the caller might say, 'Draw the four legs of a cat . . . now draw its body . . . then its head. Add a tail. Finally, give it some whiskers.' ▶ More complicated instructions might include:

'Draw the legs of a man . . . draw his head . . . now draw his body, wearing whatever you choose. Put a hat on his head. Draw his left arm with his hand in a pocket. Draw his right arm. Give him a walking stick to hold in his right hand. Put in a bus stop for him to stand by.' ▶ Players aim to make the most accurate drawing by getting the parts in the right places. ▶ At the end of each drawing, the caller judges which is the most accurate. ▶ Points are awarded according to how many players there are. If there are five players, the most accurate drawing will get 5 points, the next will get 4, . . . and so on. The least accurate drawing gets 1 point. ▶ Players take a turn each at being the caller. At the end of the game, the player with most points is the winner.

A

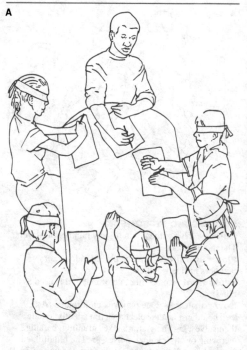

A

SQUEAK–PIGGY–SQUEAK

Number This game is fun for any number of players. The more the better.

Place and time It can be played indoors, or outdoors in fine weather.

Equipment A piece of cloth or material is used as a blindfold.

How to play ▶ One player is blindfolded (**A**).
▶ The other players select a victim silently among themselves. ▶ The victim makes grunting, barking, meowing or other animal noises. ▶ The blindfolded person tries to identify the victim from the voices. ▶ If successful, the victim becomes the blindfolded person and another player is selected to make the noises.

PASS THE RING

Number This game is for at least eight players.

Place and time It can be played indoors, or outdoors in fine weather. It is a good game to play in the dark.

Equipment A curtain ring, or something similar, is threaded onto a long piece of string and the ends of the string are tied together.

How to play ▶ Players stand in a circle (**A**). One

A

B

person stands in the centre. Another acts as a caller. The players in the circle all hold the string and pass the ring round the circle. ▶ When the caller shouts 'Stop!', the person in the centre has to guess who is holding the ring (**B**). When the guess is correct, the one with the ring goes into the centre.

Variation Players can sit a straight line in front of the guesser, holding the unjoined string and passing the ring to and fro.

MATCH PATTERNS

Number Two or more players of any age play in pairs. If there is an odd number, three can play together.

Place and time The game can be played anywhere, even in a confined space.

Equipment Each player needs ten used matches. Be sure that young children do not have access to live matches.

How to play ▶ One player of each pair makes a pattern with her ten matches while the other watches. When the pattern is complete, the partner turns her back to it and tries to reproduce the pattern exactly, including getting the match heads in the correct positions.

Variations Players can work in teams, collecting points for their team. It should be agreed how many patterns will be made. The number of matches can also be stated and more than ten can be used.

Those reproducing the pattern exactly gain 1 point. The patterns below (**A**) and those over the page (**B** and **C**) suggest some basic arrangements.

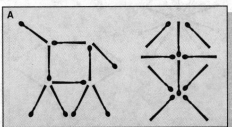

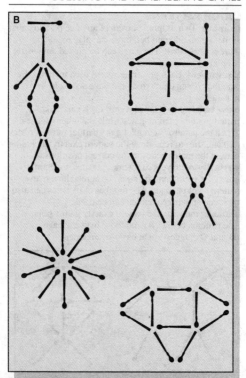

WHERE AM I?

Number Two or more players of any age can play.

Place and time The game is played indoors, or outdoors during the day, at any time of year, and in an area the players know well.

If the players are in a new area, it can be played after a visit to find their way around the new place.

How to play ▶ One player is chosen to act as the navigator. Beginning from a given starting point, such as the steps of the local museum (**A**), he describes a route round the area, referring to landmarks known to the other players (**B** and **C**). ▶ Upon arriving at his destination (**D**) he asks 'where am I?' ▶ The first to answer correctly takes the next turn as the navigator.

I begin by an old train
(Railway Museum)

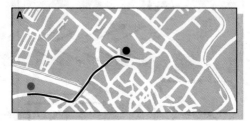

I walk to the large
religious building
(York Minster)

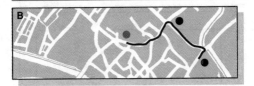

I walk to a city gate
(Monk Bar)

I pass an old inn
(Black Swan)

I pass a portrait of a Viking
(Jorrick Centre)

I keep walking till I cross a
small river and stop by a grave.
Where am I?

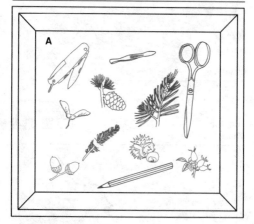

COLLECTION TRAY

Number Any number of any age can play.

Place and time The game is for indoors, or outdoors in fine weather.

Equipment A variety of objects is needed for this memory game. These might be, for example, stamps, coins, seeds, flowers, buttons, small souvenirs, badges, tickets, trinkets, nuts and bolts, screws, nails, pins, clips, etc. You also need a watch or clock, a tray and a cover for the tray, such as a towel. Each player needs a pencil and paper.

How to play ▶ Players sit in a circle. A selection of the objects is placed on the tray (**A**), which is placed in

B

the centre of the circle (**B**). Players may not touch the tray or the objects. They look at the objects and try to remember them. ▶ The tray is then covered and players write down the items they can remember. About three minutes is allowed for this. The time depends on how many objects there are. A timer can be used, but usually players use a watch or clock. ▶ After a given time, the tray is uncovered and players exchange lists and mark them, giving 1 point for each correct item. If there are several of the same item, the number must be stated correctly – for example, six paper clips. ▶ The aim of the game is to observe and remember as many of the objects as possible.

Variations The method of presentation can be varied by passing items round the circle while players are blindfolded, so that they have to recognize objects by touch or by smell.

One player can also present objects to blindfolded players who have to identify them by the sounds they make when shaken, hit or rattled.

A poster also makes a good object for observation. It is removed and one player then asks the others questions about the information on the poster.

Many different things can be used for observation, such as pictures of people and places, maps, plans, timetables or arrangements of chess or draughts pieces on a board.

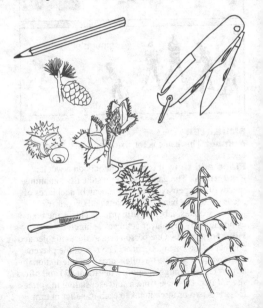

SMUGGLER
Number This game is for six or more players of any age.
Place and time It is played indoors on a wet day.
Equipment The game requires a suitcase containing pieces of inexpensive jewellery, a watch, necklaces of seeds or beads, bangles, bracelets and decorative jewellery boxes, labelled with prices. This is the booty, as prepared by the player acting as smuggler.
How to play ▶ One person acts as the smuggler and another as the customs officer. The rest of the players are travellers. ▶ The travellers are in an international airport (**A**). A smuggler approaches them (**B**) and offers several items for sale from a suitcase, stating the prices. He offers two or three items to each traveller in turn.

Players are allowed to examine the goods. ▶ Suddenly, an official approaches and the smuggler closes the case and runs away (**C**). ▶ The customs officer arrives. The travellers then have to describe to the customs officer which goods they were offered and at what price (**D**). ▶ When all descriptions are complete, the smuggler returns and the descriptions are checked for accuracy. ▶ This is a game of memory. The person who remembers the booty most accurately is the winner.
Variation Each player can take a turn as the smuggler, filling his suitcase with any collection of objects. Unusual objects help to make the game interesting.

6. Pretending games

ENVELOPE STORIES
Number The game is for a minimum of four players of any age. Players can play in teams of two or more. There should be at least two teams.
Place and time It is an excellent indoor game for a rainy day, or on a coach or train during holiday travel.
Equipment Each team needs an envelope containing an equal number of small pictures cut from magazines.

A

1. On a bridge

3. a donkey

4. eating a pineapple

2. a clown met

5. and he asked a nun to

6. help him load it onto a truck

Six is a suitable number. The pictures can be exchanged between teams after each game.

How to play ▶ Each team makes up an elaborate story around the pictures, such as those shown (**A** and **B**). (In a variation, each team takes turns to select a card, at some point in their story, and offers this card to their opponents who must continue the story incorporating the subject of the card.) Each story linking the pictures can have many elements and events other than those shown in the pictures. ▶ There is no real winner – the game is played just for fun.

B

1. A pineapple fell off

2. the back of a truck

3. onto a nun

4. who was under a bridge

5. riding a donkey

6. on her way to visit a clown

STATUES

Number More than four of any age can play.

Place and time The game can be played anywhere outdoors in dry weather.

Equipment None.

How to play ▶ One person is elected as the puller. The players stand facing the puller in a line, each with one hand outstretched (**A**). ▶ The puller first asks each one which kind of pull they want, by saying 'Do you want salt, pepper or mustard?' (a gentle, medium or a fast pull). He then pulls each player by hand out of the line in turn. ▶ The puller can swing a player round or

give him a spin on the way. Each pulled player now freezes into the position in which he was thrown, as if he were a statue (**B**). ▶ When everyone is frozen, the puller tells them what role to play. Players can each be given the same character or have different ones, such as a monster, goblin, rock star, fairy, elephant, duck, etc. ▶ When the puller says, 'Clockwork' (**C**), everyone begins to act their part. ▶ When the puller says, 'Stop', everyone must now make a statue that characterizes the parts they have played (**D**). ▶ The puller next shouts, 'Lights out', and everyone must close their eyes. ▶ The puller then has to choose which is the ugliest, funniest, prettiest pose, and so on, according to the character played. He does this by quietly going round and touching all the other players who drop out, very quietly. ▶ When the winner is left, still with eyes shut, all the other players tiptoe round and together shout, 'You are it', or some other agreed declaration (**E**). ▶ The winner becomes the new puller.

Variations The aim of the game can simply be to stay still for the longest time. Dead Lions is a version in which two or three players have to keep their faces straight despite being taunted and tickled by the others. Another version is called 'What do you want?' In this, the player is asked by the others, 'What do you want?', meaning, 'How would you like to die?' The reply is by arrow, grenade or atom bomb (or any other method of execution). The player then has to fall down as if dead. When everyone has had a turn, the winner is the one whose death scene was the most spectacular. Everyone has a vote.

E

WHAT'S MY LINE?
Number The game is for four or more of any age.
Place and time It is played indoors or outdoors in dry weather.
Equipment None.
How to play ▶ Each player secretly chooses an occupation and in turn mimes a piece of action that would be involved in doing the job. ▶ When someone thinks that she has guessed the job being mimed, she mimes another part of the job. The mimer then says if it is right or not. Players continue to add pieces of mime as they make a guess until everyone has guessed, or given up.
Variation The game can be played for points. After the mime, players ask questions that can only be answered with yes or no. Anyone can make a guess at the occupation. If they are right, they gain a point and become the next mimer.
If, after an agreed time limit, nobody has guessed correctly, the mimer gets the point and has another turn. Instead of occupations, domestic jobs and everyday activities could be used.

A

CHARADES

Number This is a game for at least eight players in two teams of four or four teams of two. Alternatively, it can be played by two or more players, with an audience of non-players. People of any age can play.

Place and time It is suitable for indoors any time, evening or day, or outdoors in warm weather.

Equipment None is essential. However, if a box of old clothes and accessories is available, it would add to the fun.

How to play ▶ Each team chooses a word with several syllables. A charade is then acted out (**A**) by

B

one or more members of the team (**B**), each part of the charade being a syllable of the word chosen. ▶ The other teams and any non-playing audience have to guess the word. ▶ The team that guesses correctly then takes its turn to play charades.

Examples of words and how they can be split up into syllables are:

Sat-is-fac-tion; i-mag-in-a-tion; ad-ven-tur-ous; ex-peri-men-tal; com-pu-ter; sys-tem-at-ic-al-ly.

Variation Some keen charade players allow names to be used as well, for example: Mar-co-Po-lo; Vin-cent-Van-Gogh; Con-stan-ti-no-ple; Liv-er-pool.

IMAGINATION STICK

Number Any number, even two, can play, challenging each other.

Place and time It can be played anywhere at any time.

Equipment You need a stick about 50cm long.

How to play ▶ Players take turns to pretend the stick is another object, such as an umbrella, walking stick, fly swatter, etc., and use it as shown (**A** and **B**). The others have to guess what it is. ▶ The one who guesses correctly has the next turn.

This is intended to be a fast game for quick thinkers.

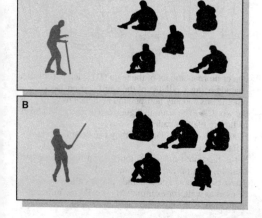

TITLES

Number The game is for two or more players, competing against each other. Any age can play.

Place and time It is played indoors any time, evening or day, or outdoors in warm weather.

Equipment None.

How to play ▶ Each player takes a turn to stand up and mime the title of a play, film, book, etc. The player begins by miming what the title is – for example, hands sweeping apart for a theatre curtain (play), cranking an imaginary camera (film) or hands held out, palms up (book). ▶ The player mimes each word separately (**A**), indicating which word it is by raising one, two or more fingers. ▶ A signal can be agreed upon to indicate words that sound like the word to be guessed – for example, putting a hand behind the ear. ▶ Everyone tries to guess the words. The first person to guess the title wins a point. Then the next player takes a turn. Examples of suitable titles include: 'The Sound of Music' (four words to mime); and 'Joseph and his Amazing Technicolour Dreamcoat' (five words to mime plus a signal for 'and', perhaps crossed fingers).

SILENT MOVIES

Number This is for two or more people in teams. Any age can play.

Place and time It is suitable for indoors or outside in dry weather.

Equipment None.

How to play ▶ Teams each decide on an activity, for example, playing baseball (**A**); throwing a caber (**B**); riding a race-horse (**C**); water-skiing; walking on the moon (**D**); and Sumo wrestling (**E**). ▶ In turn, each team acts out the activity, like a silent movie. The others have to guess exactly what they are doing.

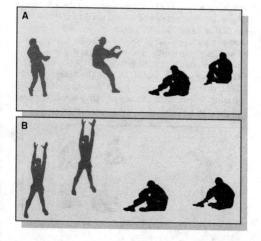

WHO AM I?

Number This is for any number of players aged nine
and upwards.

Place and time It is played indoors, or outdoors on
a warm day.

Equipment Everyone will need pen and paper on
which to note the clues. A small holdall or suitcase will
also be needed.

Preparation This game of imagination and deduction
needs some preparation beforehand. For each round of
the game, one person needs to be chosen as the clue-
maker. She secretly decides on a person (a stereotype or
relative or friend known to everyone) who she will
pretend to be. For example, she might pretend to be her
grandmother or a boy scout. She then writes out a series
of clues about 'herself', each of which is on a separate
piece of paper or card, and puts them in the holdall or
suitcase. These can be clues to 'her' preferences,
appearance and likely possessions. For example, if the
clue-maker is pretending to be her grandmother, she
might write, 'I like budgies', 'I have a blue rinse' or 'I
wear false teeth'! There is no limit to the number of
clues that may be given.

How to play ▶ The clue-maker places the open
suitcase or holdall within easy reach of all the other
players. She invites them to pick out one clue each at a
time, saying 'Who am I?' ▶ Each player notes the clue
down, puts it back and picks out a new one, which he
adds to his list. If a player has already seen a particular
clue, he is allowed to throw it back and search for a
new one. ▶ As the list of clues grows, it should
becomes easier and easier for players to guess who the

clue-maker is pretending to be. ▶ The first person to guess correctly who she is wins the round. If a player guesses incorrectly, he is out for the rest of the round.

OTHER PEOPLE'S SHOES
Number This is a game for any number of players of any age; one person could also play this game alone.
Place and time It can be played anywhere.
Equipment This depends on what is required by the action of the game.
How to play ▶ Everyone joins together to make a list of everyday activities and to collect any equipment needed to carry them out. ▶ Players then write a limitation next to each activity, for example:
peel two potatoes – one hand;
cross the room – no legs (**A**);
write your name – blindfolded (**B**);
tie your shoelaces – one hand (**C**);

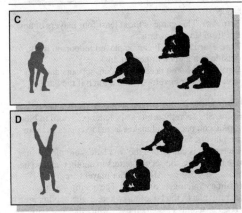

draw a map – no hands, use toes;
write a letter or poem – eyes closed;
walk on your hands – wearing shoes on your hands (**D**).
▶ Players then have to carry out the activities under
the stated limitations. ▶ Players can gain points for
themselves, competing against each other, or they can
compete in teams.
Variation Teams of two or three could extend the
range of activities – for example, putting up a tent
while blindfolded; doing a square dance or folk dance
without music; preparing and serving a meal with one
arm and hand in a sling; or miming a scene from a play.

M.I.5

Number This game is for at least four players of any age from seven upwards.

Place and time It can be played indoors at night, or outside in a garden or park at dusk.

Equipment You need paper, pen, scissors and six matchboxes or envelopes, and a torch if the game is played at dusk.

Preparation One person is chosen as the enemy agent. She secretly prints a six-letter password in block capitals on paper, and makes as many copies as there are players.

Each copy is cut up and the first letters are placed in one matchbox, the second letters in another, and so on.

How to play ▶ All the other players are M.I.5 (Military Intelligence) agents. The enemy agent secretly places the boxes anywhere in the playing area (**A**). The agents close their eyes while the boxes are put in place. ▶ First, the agents have to find the boxes (**B**) and then take one letter from each box to make up the password. While they try to do this, the enemy agent follows them around the area (**C**). ▶ Anyone who is moving when caught in the act of opening a box must surrender the last letter he has collected to the enemy. ▶ After a time limit, the enemy agent calls all the players together and the first M.I.5 agent to declare the password wins the game and becomes the next enemy agent.

Variations The password can be longer, in which case more matchboxes would be needed.

A

B

C

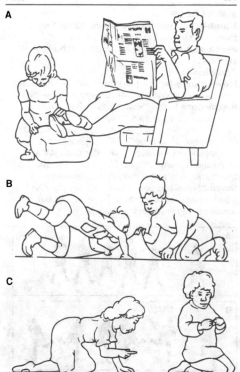

SIMON SAYS

Number Any number can play this game, four or more being the best. It is suitable for any age.

Place and time It can be played anywhere and at any time.

Equipment None.

How to play ▶ One player is chosen as Simon (**A**), who gives everyone else simple instructions. ▶ When the command begins 'Simon says . . .', it should be carried out – for example, 'Simon says "Hop" ' (**B**), 'Simon says "Sit" ' (**C**), 'Simon says "Crouch" ' (**D**), 'Simon says "Hold hands" ' (**E**), or 'Simon says "Hands above your heads" ' (**F**). But when just a command is given, without 'Simon says', it should be ignored. ▶ Any player carrying out the command incorrectly has to drop out until only one player is left, who becomes the new Simon. To get players out, Simon must give commands quickly.

C Simon says 'SIT'

D Simon says 'CROUCH'

E Simon says 'HOLD HANDS'

F Simon says 'HANDS ABOVE YOUR HEADS'

7. Challenges

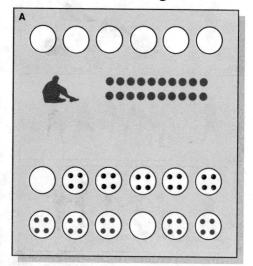

FOUR STONES
Number This game is for two players. After each
game a new player can challenge the winner.
Place and time It can be played anywhere, and is
especially suitable for a beach when the weather is fine.
Equipment Each player needs 20 small stones.
How to play ▶ Players sit opposite each other and

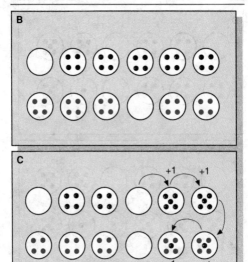

each player draws six circles in a line in the sand (**A**). ▶ Players put four stones in five of their circles (**B**), leaving a circle empty. ▶ Players decide who begins and the first player now picks up the four stones from one of her own circles. ▶ She moves along her own line of circles in one direction and then along her opponent's line in the opposite direction, placing a

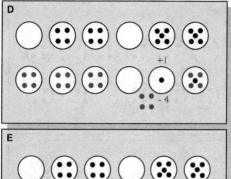

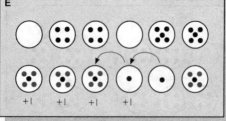

stone in each circle (**C**). ▶ If there are already stones in the circle in which she places her last stone, she leaves her stone in that circle and picks up the four stones there (**D**). Then she continues along the line putting one stone into each circle (**E**). The turn ends when she puts a stone into a circle that is empty. ▶ Her opponent then has his turn, starting from one of his own circles. ▶ As the stones are distributed, players collect them as winnings when they place a stone in a circle that only

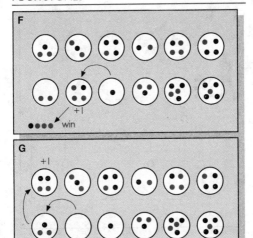

contains three stones (**F**), making the total four. The
player keeps all four stones as winnings, puts them
aside, and continues playing as before (**G**). ▶ A player
may begin her turn of play from one of her opponent's
circles when all her own circles are empty. ▶ The aim
of the game is to collect as many fours as possible and
to prevent the opponent from collecting any. The game
ends when only four stones remain in the game. The
winner is the player who has collected most fours.

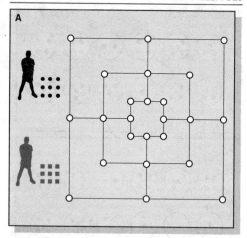

NINE MEN'S MORRIS

Number This game is for two players of any age, but not too young.

Place and time It can be played indoors, or anywhere outdoors where it is possible to mark out a playing board on the ground, using rope or chalk, or by scratching with a stone. Alternatively, the game can be played on a table, with the playing board marked out on paper.

Equipment Each player needs nine 'men' which can be skittles, bottles, pebbles, seeds, counters or anything else that can easily be moved around. Each player's

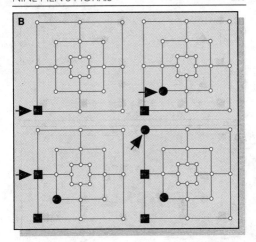

men should be different in colour or shape from those of the other players.

Preparation Mark out a playing area on the ground about 12 paces square as shown in the diagram (**A**). Twenty-four small circles should be drawn and connected by straight lines. The circles on which the players' 'men' are first placed are called the 'homes'.

How to play ▶ The game is played in three stages.

▶ *Stage one.* Players toss a coin to see who begins. The first player places one of his men on any of the circles. The second player then puts one of his men on a different circle (**B**). Players continue to place their men,

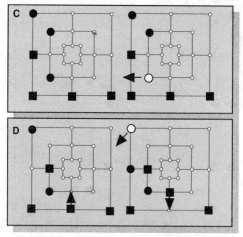

one at a time, and in turn, on the circles. ▶ Each player aims to get three men in a straight row, either vertically or horizontally. This row is called a 'mill' (**C**). When a player achieves this, he may remove one of his opponent's men from the board (but not one that is part of a mill). ▶ **Stage two.** When a player has placed all his men on the board, he can make one of two possible moves. He can break and reform his mills by moving one of his men to an adjacent empty circle. Then, on his next turn, he can move it back. This allows him to remove one of his opponent's men as technically, he has made a new mill. (**D**). ▶ Alternatively, he can

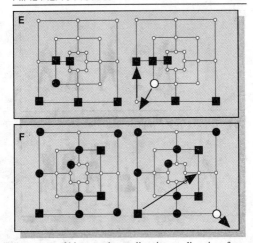

move one of his men along a line, in any direction, from one space to the next along that line. ▶ A man can only be moved one space in each turn, and can only be moved to a vacant space. As before, when players make a row of three men, they remove one of their opponent's men (**E**). ▶ *Stage three.* When a player has only three men remaining on the board, he may use his turn to make a jump from 'home' to any other vacant space on the board, instead of sliding, offering more opportunities to make a mill (**F**). The game continues until one player has only two men left and the other player wins.

DISGUISES

Number Any number of any age over about eight can play.

Place and time It is suitable for indoors or out walking, on a picnic or at the beach. It is best in warmer weather, if outdoors.

Equipment None.

How to play ▶ Each player secretly chooses a living person known to all the other players (**A**). The person can be local or someone in entertainment, for example. Players then toss for who goes first. ▶ The first player gives clues as to the identity of his chosen person by saying, 'I am not really Jack/Jill (the player's real

C 'I RIDE A HORSE'

D 'I APPEAR IN MOVIES'

name) at all; this is only my disguise. I will give you five clues as to who I am . . .' ▶ The player gives five clues (**B**), (**C**) and (**D**), such as age, sex, occupation, nationality, famous saying, hair style, accent etc. ▶ When the clues have been given, each of the guessing players can ask one question to which the answer has to be yes or no only. ▶ At any point, a player can make a guess at the person's name, but each player can have only two guesses. ▶ The first player to guess correctly wins and takes the next turn. ▶ If nobody guesses correctly, the same player declares the name and chooses who has the next turn.

BUCKING BRONCOS

Number This game is for any number matched in pairs for height and strength (**A**).

Place and time It is best played outside in summer, and on grass or sand. It is not suitable for playing on a hard surface.

Equipment None.

How to play ▶ One of a pair is the horse and the other the rider (**B**). The aim is for the bucking bronco to unseat her rider. If several pairs are playing, the game

can go on until only one rider remains on her horse and is the winner. ▶ The pairs then change places (**C**), the rider becoming horse and horse becoming rider, and the game is played out again. ▶ Players may want to change partners for a third and fourth round.

Variations Pairs may prefer to challenge each other, with riders trying to unseat each other, using soft cushions (**D**). This game is popular with boys and girls, and a knockout competition can be devised if there are enough players.

SOAPBOX CORNER

Number This game is for any number of players. It is best for those who can stand up and talk in front of an audience.

Place and time The game is played indoors in private or outdoors where some shouting will not disturb other people.

Equipment You will need a strong wooden box, stool or rock to stand on as a soapbox.

Preparation Everyone is given a few minutes to think up a subject they feel strongly about – for example, pocket money, starving people or dogs.

How to play ▶ Players decide who shall speak first. ▶ The speaker stands on the soapbox (**A**) and speaks on her subject for three minutes. Her aim is to convince the others of her point of view. Heckling is allowed. ▶ When all players have spoken, a vote is taken as to which speech was the most convincing.

CONFUSION

Number Three, six or nine players can play in three teams. One non-playing person acts as instructor and referee.

Place and time The game is played outdoors on the beach or in a field, at any time. It can also be played indoors in a large hall.

Equipment What is needed depends upon the instructions given. In the examples given here, three or four chairs are used if playing indoors, and two or three small buckets or plastic cartons if playing on a sandy beach.

How to play ▶ The players form teams of three (**A**). Each team is secretly given a set of instructions by the non-player. The teams must not know each other's

B team 1 makes sand castles

C team 2 fills buckets

D team 3 buries buckets

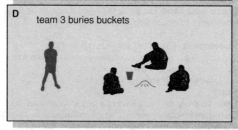

instructions. ▶ The aim is to carry out the instructions within a set time limit after the non-player gives the signal.

▶ Example of instructions for an indoor game:

Team 1 Sit on chairs in the centre of the hall.
Team 2 Place all chairs upright at side of hall.
Team 3 Turn all chairs upside down.

▶ Example of instructions for a beach game:

Team 1 Use buckets to build sand castles (**B**).
Team 2 Fill buckets with water (**C**).
Team 3 Bury buckets in the sand (**D**).

The instructions for each team cannot all be carried out successfully (**E**). Therefore, if teams are evenly matched, there will be no winning team.

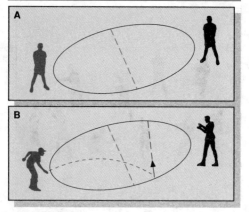

TERRITORIES

Number Two or more players aged nine or over can play in pairs.

Place and time It is played anywhere outdoors in dry weather, or indoors where there is space to mark out a circle about 1 metre in diameter.

Equipment Something is needed, such as chalk, to mark the circle and draw a line across the centre of it. You also require an item with a point, such as a pen or a flat pebble with an arrow marked on it.

Preparation A circle with a line through the middle is needed for each pair of players. Each player claims half the circle as his territory (**A**).

How to play ▶ Players toss for who should play

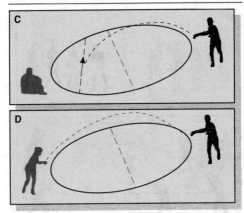

first. ▶ The players in turn throw the pen or stone into the other's territory. To do this, they must stand four paces outside the circle, anywhere opposite their own territory. ▶ The line in the circle is redrawn where the pen or stone landed (**B**) and in the direction it points. ▶ The thrower claims the larger segment as his own (**C**). ▶ Players continue throwing in turn, aiming for the opponent's new segment and attempting to make the pen or stone land in the ground in such a way as to decrease the opponent's territory. ▶ The winner is the one who makes the pen or stone land so that it lands exactly on the line of the circle (**D**), anywhere inside his opponent's segment.

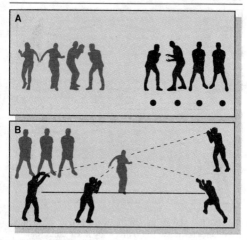

WALKING THE PLANK

Number The game is for at least eight people of similar ages in two teams (**A**).

Place and time It is played indoors in a large hall, or outdoors where there is space. It is best in dry weather, if played outdoors.

Equipment A rope about 6 or more metres long or a piece of chalk is needed to mark a line. Players also need a supply of soft balls for players to throw at each other. A minimum of one ball is needed for each member of one team.

How to play ▶ A line is marked on the ground

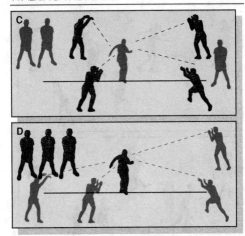

along which one team is to walk. The other team has the balls, which they throw at the walking team, attempting to knock them off-balance (**B**) and (**C**). Care must be taken not to aim at the head. ▶ The teams walk the line in turn (**D**), noting how many surviving members there were. ▶ A walking player who puts a foot on the ground off the line, or puts his foot across the line instead of along it, is out. ▶ The game continues until an agreed number of turns have taken place. Teams then total their numbers of survivors. The winning team is the one with the highest score.

CHAIN TAG

Number Any number of players of any age can play.
At least four are needed to make a good game.

Place and time The game can be played outdoors at
any time. A lot of running space is needed, but a clear
boundary must be agreed between the players before
the game begins.

Equipment None.

How to play ▶ One player is chosen as the devil

(**A**); the others are known as refugees. ▶ The devil must run and tag a refugee (**B**) by touching her. ▶ The player who has been touched must then hold hands with the devil and run with her (**C**) as she chases yet another refugee. ▶ Each refugee the devil tags joins hands to form a chain (**D**). ▶ The person at the end of the chain may also tag as the remaining refugees are chased. The devil's aim is to catch all the refugees. The last one caught becomes the new devil for the next game.

JUMPING JACK

Number The game is for two or more, but the more the better. It is for players of any age who can jump. One player acts as referee.

Place and time It is played wherever the ground or floor can withstand several people jumping up and down for a long period.

Equipment None.

How to play ▶ At the word 'Go' from a referee, everyone begins to jump up and down on the spot (**A**). Jumping should be done with both feet, which must

leave the ground together (**B**). ▶ The referee
eliminates anyone who begins to vary his jump, such as
jumping from foot to foot or resting between jumps.
Eliminated players must sit out the rest of the game
(**C**). ▶ Anyone who gets tired and stops jumping drops
out. The aim of the players is to be the one who is still
jumping after everyone else has either dropped out or
been eliminated (**D**).
If a wide age range is playing, there can be winners of
each age group, as well as an overall winner.

TUG OF WAR
Number The game is for, at best, 16 players in two
teams of 8 (**A**). Any age can take part.
Place and time It can be played outdoors on a field
or other soft ground, but not a paved area. It is suitable
at any time, even in the rain as mud seems part of the
pleasure of this challenge.
Equipment A sturdy rope about 30 metres long is
needed.
Preparation Three lines are marked parallel to each
other, 2 metres apart.
How to play ▶ First, a referee should be found. The
rope is laid at right angles across the lines, with an
equal amount of rope on both sides of the central line.

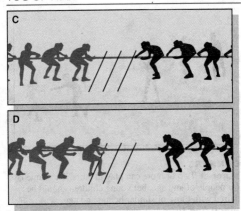

▶ Each team lines up behind its leader (**B**), next to the rope, the leaders behind their respective lines. The teams face each other. ▶ At the signal 'Take the strain' from the referee, the teams pick up the rope and hold themselves ready (**C**). ▶ The end person in each team, usually the heaviest individual, may pass the rope under one arm and over his shoulder. ▶ The team members all take the strain by holding the rope in both hands, leaning backwards with front leg straight and feet sideways to provide better resistance. ▶ The referee then gives the signal 'Go' and both teams heave on the rope as hard as they can (**D**). ▶ Each team tries to pull the opponent's leader over the central line. The team that achieves this is the winner.

CONKERS

Number Two or more can play in pairs. The game is for people of any age, but young children should be paired with those of similar height and age.

Place and time It is played indoors or outdoors during autumn.

Equipment Each player needs a ripe horse chestnut, the fruit of the tree of that name. The horse chestnut fruit is also known as a conker.

Preparation A small hole is driven through the conker with a skewer, and a shoelace or string about 60cm long is drawn through it. A knot is tied in one end of the string so that the conker will hang on the string.

How to play ▶ One player challenges another. The challenger plays first. ▶ The challenged player holds his conker string, keeping the dangling conker still, at arm's length (**A**) and at a height chosen by the challenger. ▶ The challenger wraps his string twice round his hand, holds his conker in the other hand and

takes aim, pulling his string and hitting the dangling conker with his own as hard as possible. ▶ The aim is to break the opponent's conker (**B**). ▶ When a hit is made, the other player then has his turn. A challenger is allowed up to three turns if he misses. ▶ If the strings tangle, the one who is first to shout 'Strings' has an extra turn. ▶ When one new conker breaks another new conker so that there is nothing left hanging on the string, the winning conker is called a 'one-er.' ▶ Winning conkers can add the value of the losing conker to that of their own. For example, a 'five-er' (a conker that has broken five other conkers) breaking a 'three-er' scores 1 point for winning that match and adds the loser's value, making the 'five-er' into a 'nine-er'.

Conkers can be treated to make them tougher. The new, shiny conker is called a 'straight'; a flat one is called a 'cheesie'; and one kept a year to harden is a 'yearsie'. Conkers can also be hardened by soaking in vinegar, salt and water or soda. Slow baking hardens them, too.

HOPPING

Number The game is for four or more players.

Place and time It can be played outdoors at any time. Any open space will do. Players should agree the safe zones. Note that it is dangerous to play this game in the street.

Equipment None.

Preparation Two parallel lines about a metre apart are drawn on the ground with chalk. The space between the lines represents the 'road'.

How to play ▶ One player is chosen as the 'cocker' and stands (**A**) in between the two safe zones. ▶ The players line up in one of the safe zones. The cocker stands on one leg with arms folded. She challenges any player to cross the 'road' to the other safe zone. ▶ The

player has to try to cross the central zone by hopping on one foot, with arms folded (**B**). The cocker tries to knock the player off balance. If the player puts the other foot to the ground (**C**), he has to stay in the centre with the cocker (**D**) and help her to catch the other players. ▶ If the cocker loses balance and puts her other foot to the ground, the player gets free passage across. ▶ A player who reaches the other side safely shouts 'Cockarusha' which shows it is the turn of another player to be challenged. ▶ Every time players are captured, they help to do the chasing, so it gets increasingly difficult to get across. ▶ Those who manage to do so are challenged in turn to get back to the other safe zone. ▶ The winner is the player who remains when everyone else has been captured.

TIP

Number Two or more players of any age can play.

Place and time It can be played indoors or outside in dry weather on the ground or at a table.

Equipment You need eight small objects – for example, a coin, sweet, pen, button, leaf, pebble, matchbox or marble. Place these on the ground or on a table.

How to play ▶ One person is chosen to play, and must turn away (**A**) while the others decide which is to be the forbidden object. ▶ The player turns round and

A

is invited to pick up the objects one by one (**B**). If she touches the forbidden object, everyone shouts 'Tip!', and she must return the objects to the table. ▶ The next player then has a turn, the others deciding which is the forbidden object. ▶ The player has to pick up all objects, except the forbidden one. The winner usually gets to eat the sweet as a prize and a new sweet is added.

The game can be varied by changing all the objects from time to time and increasing the number. Sometimes, two forbidden objects can be chosen.

B

SHOUT OUT

Number At least eight players, of any age, can play.

Place and time It is played indoors or outdoors on a warm, fine evening where other people will not be disturbed by an occasional shout.

Equipment The game requires some object as treasure, such as a ball or a small box. A blindfold is also needed.

How to play ▶ Players sit in a circle with one as the pirate in the centre (**A**). Another player is chosen to be the referee and he stands outside the circle in view of the players. ▶ The seated players should be at least three paces away from the pirate, who wears a blindfold. ▶ The pirate places his treasure on the ground near to him. ▶ The referee points at a player

who creeps very quietly towards the treasure. The
pirate points (**B**) in the direction of any sound he hears,
attempting to catch the creeping player. ▶ The pirate
must not swing his pointing finger in an arc but must
point towards individual directions. ▶ If the direction
hits the creeping player (**C**), the referee shouts 'Out'
and the player must return to his place in the circle. The
referee now chooses another person (**D**) to try to
capture the treasure. ▶ The player who captures the
treasure wins that round and becomes the next pirate.
▶ A new referee is chosen whenever the treasure is
captured or when everyone has had a turn.

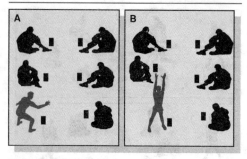

DRINK A TOAST

Number The game is for any number of players of any age.

Place and time It is played indoors or outdoors, sitting in a circle on the ground, or round a table. This is a good game to play when everyone feels like having a refreshing drink after a very active game.

Equipment You need one drink in a can or glass for each person.

How to play ▶ Each person in turn has to perform a ritual correctly before she is allowed to enjoy her drink. ▶ Players sit with their drinks and one person begins the ritual. ▶ The player stands and says, 'I drink a toast to Slippery Sue and Silly Sam as they sit on the sand at the seaside.' A different toast can be invented if the players wish, but everyone has to use the same one. ▶ The player then continues the ritual as follows:
– touches player to left with one finger;
– touches player to right with one finger;

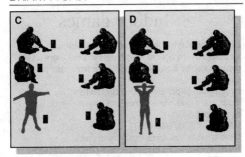

– puts right arm out to the side (**A**);
– puts both arms in the air (**B**);
– stretches arms and legs apart to either side (**C**);
– puts both hands behind head (**D**);
– bows once to the left, bows once to the right;
– picks up drink with first finger and thumb, taps her forehead once with the can and takes one sip.

The player then repeats the whole ritual again using two fingers and two bows and two taps, and taking two sips. ▶ Finally, she does it using three fingers, three bows and three taps, and taking three sips. When she has completed the whole ritual correctly, she can then sit down and enjoy the rest of her drink. ▶ The next player then begins the ritual. ▶ Anyone making a mistake in carrying out the ritual has to wait until everyone else has had their turn, and tries again. ▶ Players who are sitting waiting, or who have successfully completed their ritual, can try to distract the one performing.

The aim is finally to get your drink!

8. Indoor games

Games for playing indoors at any time during wet weather can, of course, also be played outdoors on picnics, on the beach or as a change from energetic games.

Pencils and paper are needed for the first five games; the rest are oral word games and do not require any equipment.

DRAW A SQUIGGLE

Number Any number can play in pairs.

Equipment Each player needs a pencil and a sheet of paper. A watch will be needed to time the game.

How to play ▶ Each player makes a squiggle (**A**) on his sheet of paper. Players then exchange papers and have two minutes to make something of the opponent's squiggle (**B**). ▶ The aim is ingenuity. Drawing ability does not count. ▶ A third person can be asked to judge which is the most inventive idea.

Variation Players can make five or six squiggles from which as many drawings as possible have to be made.

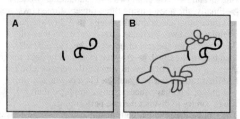

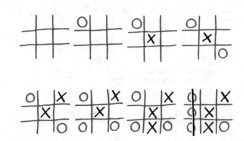

NOUGHTS AND CROSSES

Number This game is for two players.

Equipment Paper and a pencil are needed for each player.

Preparation Nine spaces are made by drawing two vertical lines crossed by two horizontal lines.

Players agree who should draw noughts ('O') and who should draw crosses ('X').

How to play ▶ One player begins, placing his O in any space. His opponent puts her X in any space. They continue to take turns to mark the spaces. ▶ The aim is to get a row of noughts or a row of crosses, in any direction – horizontally, vertically or diagonally.

▶ The player getting a line of three first is the winner. If neither gets a line, that round is a draw. ▶ Players take it in turn to go first, because the one who goes first has a slight advantage over the other.

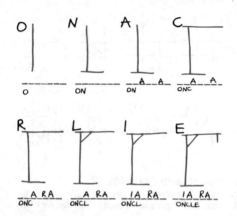

HANGMAN

Number Two or more of any age can play.

Equipment A pencil and paper are needed for each player.

Preparation One player thinks of a word and counts the number of letters in it. She then makes the same number of dashes on a piece of paper, one for each letter, and gives the others a clue – for example, another word for 'picture'.

How to play ▶ The others guess a letter in turn. If the letter is in the word, the player puts it in place, twice if it occurs twice, and so on. ▶ If the letter is not in the word, the player starts to draw the hanged man.

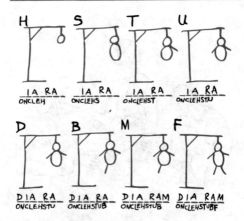

Each line in the drawing is one wrong letter. Incorrect letters are written below the dashes so everyone can see which letters have already been called.

Winning If a player guesses the word before the hanged man is complete, she is the winner and chooses the next word. If the drawing is completed before anyone guesses the word, then the player who thought up the word wins and has another turn choosing a new word.

The complete drawing of the hanged man has eleven parts. A sample sequence is shown above.

CREATING ANSWERS

Number This is a game for three or more players.

Equipment Each player needs a pencil and three pieces of paper about the size of a postcard. Children often enjoy playing several rounds of this game so more paper will be needed for each round.

Preparation The papers are numbered 1, 2 and 3. On his paper 1, each player writes a question (**A**). The more interesting the questions, the better the game will turn out to be.

On his paper 2, each player writes any word.

B

Players now fold papers 1 and 2, putting them into two piles (**B**). Both piles of paper are shuffled. Samples of questions and words are given over the page (**C** and **D**).
How to play ▶ Each player in turn takes a paper 1 and a paper 2. ▶ On his paper 3, he has to write out an answer to the question he has picked, which should include the word he has picked. The aim is to write the most creative answer. ▶ If there are only three players, then each player should write two questions on two papers numbered 1 and two words on two papers numbered 2. This gives everyone more choice.

C
- Why do worms wriggle?
- How big is the Eiffel Tower?
- What can you find at the end of a rainbow?
- If you could fly, how would you launch yourself?
- Why does the pencil always break just when you need it?
- Who is the cleverest person here?
- How will you know when the end of the world has come?
- What did Jill say when she and Jack fell down the hill?

Sample questions on paper 1

D
- HUT
- ODD
- GOOSE
- JUMPING
- DOUBLE
- FINGER
- JAM
- MAP

Sample words on paper 2

If a player had the question 'Why do worms wriggle?' and the word 'map', the answer might be, 'Worms follow microscopic maps that are kept folded up. When the map is unfolded, the paper is wavy, so the worm thinks it has to wriggle, following the folds on the map!' With plenty of imagination, this game can be very enjoyable. There are no winners or losers.

A

BLACKBERRIES

B

BRING LAMP AND CHISEL STOP

KNOW BEST ENTRY ROUTE STOP

REST IS EASY STOP SID

TELEGRAMS

Number Any number of players can join in.

Equipment A pencil for each player and two pieces of paper are needed.

Preparation Each player writes down a word of twelve letters (**A**) – it could be the name of a person, an object or a place.

How to play All the papers on which the words are written are folded up, mixed and placed in a central pile. ▶ Each player selects a paper, unfolds it and begins his telegram. The message must contain twelve words, make sense, and each word of the telegram must begin with each letter of the selected word (**B**).

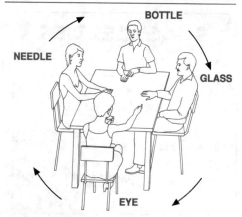

ASSOCIATIONS

Number Two or more players of any age can join in.
Equipment None.
How to play ▶ Players sit in a circle. One person begins by saying any noun, for example, bottle.
The next person must immediately say an associated word, for example, glass. ▶ The next player quickly makes an association, for example, eye, and so on. Anybody who hesitates, or who gives a word which everyone else thinks is not a proper association, is out of the game. ▶ Players continue to make associations in turn round and round the circle.
The winner is the person who stays in the game the longest.

ABC

Number Two or more players, in two teams, can play.

Equipment Pencils and paper are needed for each team.

How to play ▶ At an agreed start, both teams try to write down a list of objects with initials that are the letters of the alphabet. Usually the letters X and Z are ignored. The objects must all be in the room where play is taking place, including items in the pockets of players. Examples might include apple, bone, cash, door, etc. ▶ When a team is satisfied with the list it has made, the team members shout 'Stop.' All writing must stop at this point. ▶ The teams now compare their lists:
– any item that is on both lists is struck off;
– any item that a team cannot show to be present in the room is struck off;
– any item that is incorrectly named is struck off.
▶ The teams then total their lists of remaining objects.
▶ The teams then get together again to make a second alphabetical list of objects, but they must not use any object that was already included on either team's first list. ▶ Again, the teams compare and count their scores. ▶ Teams then make a third attempt, this list being harder to complete because objects that were on the first two lists of either team will have been struck off. ▶ When teams have compared their third lists and counted scores, they add their scores for all three lists.
▶ The team with the bigger score is the winner.

Variation If a watch is available, the rounds of the game can be timed to two minutes, which puts the players under pressure of time.

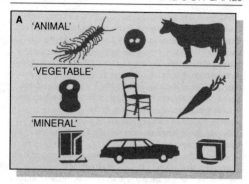

ANIMAL, VEGETABLE OR MINERAL

Number Two players of any age can play individually or in two teams.

Equipment None.

How to play ▶ One player begins by thinking of an object which he describes to the others as animal, vegetable or mineral (**A**), for example, (cat) animal; (glass bottle) mineral; (wooden spoon) vegetable. Sometimes the object may fall into two categories or all three, for example, (violin) vegetable and animal; (hammer) vegetable and mineral; (our local library) animal, vegetable and mineral. ▶ He also tells the players how many words are involved, excluding the words 'a,' 'an,' or 'the.' ▶ The players have to try and find out the object by asking a question in turn.
▶ When 20 questions have been asked, the game is

finished. ▶ The questions can only be answered with 'yes,' 'no' or 'don't know.' 'Is it large or small?' cannot, of course, be answered by 'yes' or 'no', but 'Is it large?' is a correct question because the answer can be 'yes' or 'no'.

It is best to ask general questions first to get a lead into the right direction. Examples of suitable questions include: 'Is it living?' 'Is it useful?' 'Could I wear it?' The player who is first to guess the object correctly is the winner and leads the next round by thinking of another object. ▶ If nobody guesses before twenty questions have been asked, the first player announces what the object was and can choose another object for the next round.

Variation Instead of thinking of an object, the first player thinks of a person and an object that is associated with that person. The person could be fact or fiction, known or unknown, for example, queen and country, fireman and hose, singer and microphone, Jack and well.

The other players have to guess the person and the object in 30 questions.

I LIKE MY SISTER

Number The game is for two or more players, of any age, each playing for herself.

Equipment None.

How to play ▶ Players sit in a circle. ▶ One player begins the game by saying 'I like my sister because she's . . .', filling in the end of the sentence with a word beginning with A, the first letter of the alphabet. ▶ The

next player, going clockwise round the circle, then says 'I like my sister because she's . . .', this time completing the sentence with a word beginning with B.

▶ The next player now takes a turn, using a word beginning with C, and so on round the circle.

▶ Players must not stop and think when it is their turn, but must complete their statement instantly, using the correct letter of the alphabet. Anyone who pauses or who uses a letter of the alphabet out of sequence must sit out the rest of the game. ▶ Play continues round the circle until an agreed time limit is up or until only one player remains in the game. That player is the winner.

Variations In another version, players can begin their statements with a different phrase each time. For example, the first player could say, 'I like my sister because she's . . .'; the next player could say, 'She lives in a . . . town'; the next player could say, 'Her name is . . .'; and so on.

Another variation requires players to use verbs (action words) instead of adjectives (descriptive words). The game is played as above, but players go round the circle saying, 'I like my sister; I want to . . . (with) her', filling in the missing word with a word beginning with A, then B, then C, and so on. Again, any player who pauses or who uses a letter of the alphabet out of sequence must sit out the rest of the game.

Sample words Lists of words you can use beginning with each letter of the alphabet are shown on the following spread. These are just a sample; there are many more that can be used. Usually, players pass on the letters X and Z, as fewer words begin with those letters, but including them adds challenge to the game.

Adjectives for 'I like my sister because she's . . .

A	attractive, athletic, alluring, appreciative
B	bashful, beautiful, brainy, burlesque
C	charming, cute, courteous, courageous
D	dainty, dextrous, daring, different
E	eccentric, energetic, errant, extravagant
F	fair, fun, flamboyant, forceful
G	gallant, gorgeous, groovy, generous
H	happy, hilarious, hearty, humble
I	ingenious, illustrious, imaginative, intelligent
J	jaunty, jolly, jubilant, joyful
K	keen, kind, knowledgeable
L	lenient, loyal, lively, lavish
M	mad, mischievous, modish, mysterious
N	natty, notorious, noble, nice
O	obedient, optimistic, open-minded, outspoken
P	polite, patient, prestigious, profound
Q	quiet, qualitative, queenly, quick
R	rebellious, resolute, resourceful, responsible
S	silly, sagacious, sedate, skilful
T	timid, thin, thoughtful, tolerant
U	upstanding, understanding, unselfish
V	veracious, virtuous, vivacious, valiant
W	warm, wholesome, wise, wonderful
X	X-rayable
Y	young, youthful
Z	zany, zealous

Verbs for 'I like my sister; I want to . . . (with) her'

- **A** act, applaud, arrive
- **B** bake, boogie
- **C** cook, chatter, commune
- **D** drink, dance, dig
- **E** eat, embroider
- **F** fly, feast
- **G** gamble, gallop
- **H** hiccup, hop
- **I** indulge, iron
- **J** jump, juggle
- **K** kowtow, kick
- **L** limbo, lunch
- **M** meet, monopolize
- **N** nudge, nickname
- **O** oversee, obstruct
- **P** play, protect
- **Q** question, qualify, quell
- **R** read, recommend
- **S** speak, sing, strengthen
- **T** talk, train, travel
- **U** understand, uplift
- **V** visit, vaccinate
- **W** watch, wrestle, work
- **X** x-ray, xerox
- **Y** yawn, yell, yank, yodel
- **Z** zap, zoom

FIZZ BUZZ

Number This game is for two or more players, but not the very young who are not yet familiar with numbers.

Equipment None.

How to play ▶ There are three variations of this game: Fizz, Buzz and Fizz Buzz. ▶ In each variation, players call numbers in turn and in the correct order. The first player begins by calling 'One'; the next calls 'Two', the next 'Three', and so on.

Variation one: Fizz When a player reaches the number 7, a multiple of 7 or a number with 7 in it, he must say 'Fizz' instead of that number.

Variation two: Buzz When a player reaches the number 5, a multiple of 5 or a number with 5 in it, he must say 'Buzz' instead of that number.

Variation three: Fizz Buzz This is a combination of Fizz and Buzz, that is, saying 'Fizz' for every 7 and 'Buzz' for every 5. In addition, when a number contains both 5 and 7, the player must call 'Fizz Buzz' or 'Buzz Fizz'. For example, 57 contains a 5 and a 7, so the player would call 'Buzz Fizz'. The number 35 contains 5 and is a multiple of 7 and 5, so the player would call 'Buzz Fizz Buzz'.

Players making a wrong call are out. The last player left is the winner.

I SPY

Number Two or more players can join in.

Equipment None.

How to play ▶ One person starts as the spy by secretly choosing an object that is visible to the players, who may have to turn around to see it but do not need to move about. ▶ The spy says, 'I spy with my little eye something beginning with . . .', giving the initial letter or letters of the object. For example, J for jug, H for handbag, GC for green chair, RR for red rose. If there are several of the same object in the room, such as a bunch of red roses, the players have to guess which individual rose was spied. ▶ The first player to correctly guess the object becomes the new spy.

Variations Very young children may like to choose colours by saying, for example, 'I spy with my little eye something red.'

Older children may like to spy several letters by choosing objects in their place, for example, 'I spy a GA in a WB' (a green apple in a wooden bowl).

COLLINS GEM

Other Gem titles that may interest you include:

Gem Travel Games
An indispensable help in keeping children amused
on journeys **£3.50**

Gem Card Games
A handy guide that explains the rules and strategies
of play for a wide variety of popular family card
games **£3.50**

Gem Card Games 2
A selection of over 80 competitive card games to be
played for stakes **£3.50**

Gem Games for One
A compact guide to over 100 games and activities to
play by yourself **£3.50**

Gem Pub Games
A fascinating collection of traditional and modern
public house pastimes **£3.50**

COLLINS GEM

Bestselling Collins Gem titles include: